A New in Beloved Community:

Stories with the Power to Transform Us

Linda Lee, General Editor
Safiyah Fosua, Consulting Editor

Abingdon Press
Nashville

A NEW DAWN IN BELOVED COMMUNITY:
STORIES WITH THE POWER TO TRANSFORM US

This book is printed on acid-free, recycled paper.

ISBN 978-1-426-75840-9

12 13 14 15 16 17 18 19 20 21—10 9 8 7 6 5 4 3 2 1

MANUFACTURED IN THE UNITED STATES OF AMERICA

But now in Christ Jesus you who were once far off have been brought near by the blood of Christ. For He is our peace; in his flesh he has made both groups into one and has broken down the dividing wall, that is, the hostility between us. . . . So then you are no longer strangers and aliens, but you are citizens with the saints and also members of the household of God.
(Ephesians 2:13-14, 19)

Contents

Preface

"It is incumbent upon the bearers of this vision of a beloved community to do whatever we can today to hasten the day of a just world with peace. This is our hope, our prayer and our commitment."
From a "Statement of the United Methodist Council of Bishops," 2010

This book comes from a vision born out of the work of the Racism Task Force of the United Methodist Council of Bishops. The Task Force was created some time ago to assist the Council to address issues related to race and relationship in the church. During the 2008–2012 quadrennium, the focus of the Task Force shifted to building beloved community within the Council and assisting the council to include cultural competency as part of its work as a learning community. As United Methodists began to deal with the reality that we are a global church, the Task Force also desired to speak to the impact of racism and racial discrimination around the globe and to offer a vision for possible solutions. The goal was to provide a tool that could help create cultural competency in the church, beginning in the Council, which would assist the church to build beloved community in ways that would transform the world.

This vision was shared with a small group of very brave and care-filled persons who were willing to share their stories. At great personal and possibly social or professional risk, they have spoken their truths, experiences, offered suggestions for action and visions for hope. They have "sung their songs" to a new dawn of beloved community in the twenty-first century.

Each writer was asked to write ten to twenty pages based on the following:

1. Description of their own community (culture, tribe, people, race)
   a. Distinctive values, family, community rituals, practices, foods, cosmology, theology
   b. Impact of racism/white supremacy, colonization, tribalism with two to three examples
1. Theological or biblical descriptions of people living in beloved community
2. Biblical examples of broken community
3. Descriptions of how brokenness was healed in biblical examples
4. Specific examples of contemporary solutions
5. Impediments
6. Reasons for hope

Our hope was that this work would contribute to making it possible for human beings to live in mutual regard and authentic peaceful coexistence throughout our connection and the world.

The original intention was to include one writer from each of the racial-ethnic constituencies of our denomination. For various reasons, all those asked were not able to participate at this time. Some who began were not able to complete their work. However, those who endured have offered heart and soul work, which we offer together as a gift to our beloved church with the hope that the intention of building beloved community and suggesting practical solutions will be useful and transformative.

Thank You

Thank you to the writers who so faithfully and honestly responded to a call from God, to pour your soul into this offering to our beloved denomination. We thank Mr. Ray Buckley, Rev. Dr. J. Kabamba Kiboko, Rev. Dr. David Maldonado, Dr. Åsa Nausner, Rev. Dr. Elaine Robinson, Rev. Dr. Rosetta Ross, and Rev. Dr. Samuel J. Royappa. May you be blessed in the giving and those who read be blessed in the receiving.

Thank you to our consulting editor, Rev. Dr. Safiyah Fosua, who gave of time and energy from the depths of her being in the midst of her own time of transition.

Thank you to our readers and others who gave us input, Barbara Dick for additional editing support, Dan Dick for reading, Neil Alexander, Mary Catherine Dean and The United Methodist Publishing House, the Racism Task Force of the Council of Bishops, and all those who supported, prayed for, and assisted with this project.

Thanks to God. May this word not come back to you empty, but accomplish the purpose for which you sent it forth.

INTRODUCTION

Becoming Beloved Community: Stories for a New Dawn

Linda Lee

The Vision

More than half a century ago, a man named Martin Luther King, Jr. spoke to the souls of hundreds of thousands of people around the globe.

He ignited new hope as he articulated the vision that human beings do indeed embody the capacity to live together in what he described as "beloved community." King was not the first person to coin this phrase, but he was the one in the twentieth century who gave many the hope that harmonious and equitable human coexistence was a real possibility.

The vision was of a world in which human beings would choose to regard one another based on the "content of their character" rather than the "color of their skin." This vision was of a world in which people would choose the path of non-violence for societal change rather than domination and violence. King's vision was of a world in which the resources of the planet were shared with equity so that the basic needs of all human beings could be met. It was a world in which power was determined by moral and ethical standards that prioritize both the love of Christ and the needs of the vulnerable. In this vision of the world God's love is supreme and the unity of the human race was understood by all.

King said:

But the end is reconciliation; the end is redemption; the end is the creation of the beloved community. It is this type of spirit and this type of love that can transform opposers into friends. It is this type of understanding goodwill that will transform the deep gloom of the old age into the exuberant gladness of the new age. It is this love which will bring about miracles in the hearts of men.[1]

This vision of beloved community continues to speak to our souls. Though voiced many years ago, we have not yet achieved it, so the vision and the hope it offers linger within us.

Beloved Community is a place where we belong, we are safe, we are welcome. It is that place where people of every nation, culture, language, color, gender, gender preference, class, condition, and status, are honored, respected, and included. Beloved Community is the place where working for the common good is more important than personal gain or personal power. It is the place where truth is spoken in love and conflict is resolved nonviolently and restoratively. In the Beloved Community God's love is supreme: in the beloved community the world as we know it is turned upside down. These words from Isaiah express the dawn of the new day.

The wolf shall live with the lamb, the leopard shall lie down with the kid, the calf and the lion and the fatling together, and a little child shall lead them. (Isa. 11:6)

There are people around the globe in communities, congregations, and organizations working together to create and to build beloved communities. Each context gives birth to a different expression of this sacred way of being in the world.

A Starting Point

Each effort to create beloved community holds one thing in common: the ultimate requirement of engaging with the people gifted to us wherever we may be. Whether we are in familiar and comfortable territory or in places unfamiliar to us, engagement is the key. The optimal way to build community is face to face, over time—a very, very long time. Building community requires spaces in which we listen and hear, feel and begin the process of fully being present with another human being. It is in engaging fully with another that we, if we are willing, enter their story. And as we allow ourselves to be impacted, a form of communion happens—Community.

In the dominant cultures, this kind of engagement, with those perceived to be different can lead to a profound and sometimes frightening "epiphany." Jim Perkinson writes,

> The key is depth-experience and a new kind of speaking, born of shaking, in which the heretofore "unutterable takes form and is known, if only imperfectly and provisionally, within the caesura or empty moment." (Masciandaro, xvi)
>
> And what is that caesura or gap? Sooner or later in the crucible of interracial encounter, whites are faced with facing the tragedy of race in the nakedness of a dark face. What threatens to appear, if such an epiphany is not easily banished by easy explanation, is "death," a mini-apocalypse of whiteness that alone can confer the blindness through which, paradoxically, we [white people] begin to see.[2]

Yet, for people of all cultures and languages, all tribes and lands, true encounter with the one who has been "other," antithesis, or enemy is the beginning of communion. And of the possibility for beloved community.

This book is the result of a vision to offer the stories of a few people, in their own words, out of their own truth and experience. The writers have risked their very being in the things which are shared here. It is not intended to be a quick read, but rather an immersion in the truth of another until we are absorbed by it. Immersion can bring us to the point of weeping with, exploring with, and hoping with the other. In receiving each person who has written, we will also encounter ourselves and God. This book is one opportunity to listen, to hear, and then to confess the truth of our own hearts.

But it is not only the stories that call for our hearing. In these pages simple, practical, doable actions are also suggested. Creating beloved community requires more than reading, or empathizing, or staying in our own safe places and praying or sending money.

It is our hope that receiving these stories will awaken the stories within the reader that will transform heart and soul. We pray for a stirring within to take one step never taken before toward the creation of beloved community. We believe that as each of us shares our story, a word of truth is spoken into the universe, penetrating the illusions that have guided social and religious history. Those things that are not true, and never have been, will be recognized and released. One person, one story, one action at a time, the truth of our "preciousness" in God's sight will be experienced. We believe that if enough hearts and souls are transformed, it will impact human relationship in every place and be part of a trajectory toward true Beloved Community for all of humanity.

Personal Interest

As a woman of African descent in the United States, I am personally acquainted with discrimination, marginalization, and invisibility. I've experienced the indignity of being followed around in department stores and airports because my skin color made me "suspicious" in the eyes of the follower. I have been insulted in some of the small towns I've visited by being asked, "What are *you* doing here?" I've experienced the terror of the realization than I can always be immediately targeted because the color of my skin makes it impossible to go unnoticed. In addition to personal experiences as lay and clergyperson in the church, I have gained great insight into institutional racism.[3] I found the following to be true

> Although racism may be heightened and amplified by intentionally racist personnel, the depth of the power of institutionalized racism is in its structural capacity to be self-perpetuating as though an institution has a life of its own.[4]

In the midst of this new understanding of institutional racism, I had the privilege of coming together, over the years, with people of several races and cultures. Together we saw a need to do something to create new and authentic community in the church and through the church, in the world. The beloved community, which Martin Luther King Jr. described, lived, and died for, was a symbol and a banner that kept hope alive for decades.

My parents taught me that we are all children of God. They taught me that no one was "better" than me and that I was not "better" than anyone else. They taught me that we are to respect all people because we are created in the image of God.

John Wesley, the founder of Methodism understood the world to be his parish and left for all Methodists the legacy of offering Christ to people of every culture and station in life.[5]

Biblical inspiration also guided my way:

> But now in Christ Jesus you who were once far off have been brought near by the blood of Christ. For he is our peace; in his flesh he has made both groups into one and has broken down the dividing wall, that is, the hostility between us. He has abolished the law with its commandments and ordinances, that he might create in himself one new humanity in place of the two, thus making peace, and might reconcile both groups to God in one body through the cross, thus putting to death that hostility through it. (Eph. 2:13-16)

That was great news to me! It meant beloved community was already done in God's realm! There is one humanity. The dividing walls, the hostilities between us are broken down. We are reconciled to God. We are one body. Our task is to figure out how to live into this reality created for us in and by Christ Jesus.

And so it was that I joined the multitudes who believe that it really is possible to become and to build beloved community. People from around the globe have already been on this journey for centuries.

This collection of stories is offered as one more way to assist us to engage the tellers and the spirit of these stories and to let them speak to us new possibilities for realizing the creation of beloved community.

Singing to a New Dawn

> It is a little dark still, but there are warnings of day, and somewhere out of the darkness a bird is singing to the dawn. (Paul Lawrence Dunbar, 1903)

The cover and subtitle of this book were inspired by the above quote. In researching its context, the following information came to light.

In 1903 Poet Paul Lawrence Dunbar wrote an essay entitled "Representative American Negroes."[6] In it he reflected on what it

took to be among those who "achieved something for the betterment of his race rather than for the aggrandizement of himself."
This was important because the time in which he wrote was one of
great vulnerability for people of African descent, for other people
of color in the United States, and for some people of European
descent. It was a grievous time in human history when the conver-
gence of belief in "whiteness" as supreme, fear of insufficient
resources for all, and the North American and European ideology
of being "chosen" by God to rule the world resulted in a lethal trajectory for people and nations of color not yet fully redirected, even
today.

In the United States at the time Dunbar's essay was written, this
reality was being lived out through social tensions following the
emancipation of enslaved Africans.

The Jim Crow system emerged toward the end of the historical
period called Reconstruction during which Congress enacted laws
designed to order relations between Southern whites and newly
freed blacks, and to bring the secessionist states back into the
Union. Southern whites felt profoundly threatened by increasing
claims by African Americans for social equity and economic opportunity. In reaction, white-controlled state legislatures passed laws
designed to rob blacks of their civil rights and prevent blacks from
mingling with their "betters" [whites] in public places.[7]

In this climate, white mob violence such as lynching, sexual
harassment of female employees (especially domestic workers) by
white male employers, public insult and verbal attack, and abuse
of power by employers toward their workers were common. Most
lynchings from the late nineteenth century through the mid-twentieth century were of African Americans in the Southern states.
However, Latinos, the Chinese, Native Americans, and some
whites were also victims of this terror.[8]

"Scientific" writings, later discredited, described the superiority
of the white "race" and the increasing inferiority of peoples of color
as skin tone darkened. This "evidence" allowed justification for
violence against people of color to go without consequence and in
fact to sometimes be supported by law.[9] Colonial powers continued to occupy Africa and other indigenous nations, stripping them
of natural resources. Genocide and other forms of violence were
common.[10]

Indeed this was a time in human history during which there was little to "sing" about.

The representative Negro for Dunbar was the one, who, in the face of injustice, abuse, and intentional harm, was able to stay focused on the dawn of a new day that always comes, no matter how long or dark the night. The representative Negro was able to continue to work toward a common good and hold on to the vision of and the hope for what we call today, "beloved community."

The writers of this book have sung their songs to the hope of a new dawn of beloved community in the twenty-first century.

Twenty-first Century Realities

In the twenty-first century, during the first term of the first president of the United States with African heritage, the Southern Poverty Law Center (SPLC) reported the growth of hate groups by 55 percent in 2011 as the numbers increased from 824 groups in 2010 to 1,274 in 2011. Mark Potok, senior fellow at the SPLC and editor of the Spring 2012 report, writes:

> The dramatic expansion of the radical right is the result of our country's changing racial demographics, the increased pace of globalization, and our economic woes."[11]

In the twenty-first century there are those, like Ingrid Huygens, who

> consider globalization as a form of ongoing colonialism, open to the same criticism that it relies on an instrumental racism and European cultural supremacy as ideological supports. . . .
>
> These ideologies are the building blocks for a contemporary version of a colonial 'commonsense' that colonizer groups in modern societies draw upon for everyday decisions. Such 'common sense' continues to see indigenous people as an enemy and assertions of their collective rights as primitive impediments to a worldwide capitalism.[12]

Others believe there is a twenty-first-century Jim Crow in the prison-industrial complex that marginalizes and deprives U.S. citizens of basic human rights for life for nonviolent crimes. With widely disproportionate numbers of young men and increasingly young women of color filling privatized prisons, the impact on communities of color is devastating. Michelle Alexander writes,

> This larger system, referred to here as mass incarceration, is a system that locks people not only behind actual bars in actual prisons, but also behind virtual bars and virtual walls—walls that are invisible to the naked eye but function nearly as effectively as Jim Crow laws once did at locking people of color in a permanent second-class citizenship.[13]

Still others, in the church and in the society report experiences that verify that presence does not equate to participation or access.

Yet, in the twenty-first century, the quest for human equity, civil rights, and beloved community has been expressed through the non-profit and religious sectors as well as grassroots "Occupy Movements" in the United States and their predecessor movements in other parts of the globe.

People have come together to address concerns, such as the need for employment for young people, narrowing the gap between the wealthy and the poor, curbing the rising costs of living, accessible health care for all persons (especially the most vulnerable), women's rights, social and political discourse, and equity for people of all nations and colors.

The Berlin Wall has been replaced by a compelling vision of reconciliation and world peace. Apartheid has been dismantled in South Africa. People of color are present in roles in society and in the church heretofore denied them. As CEOs, medical professionals, scientists, construction contractors, educators, clergy, and lay leaders in mainline denominations, the gifts, experiences, and perspectives of diverse constituencies are available. And, there are still voices that need to be included, stories that need to be told and heard, wounds that need to be healed. Today by learning the stories of others and learning our own stories to share, we can change the trajectory of human relationship around the globe from one which continues to divide and to objectify, to one in which the work of being and building beloved community becomes reality.

Beloved Community

Revelations 7:9-12 offers us one vision for beloved community;

> After this I looked, and there was a great multitude that no one could count, from every nation, from all tribes and peoples and languages, standing before the throne and before the Lamb, robed in white, with palm branches in their hands. They cried out in a loud voice, saying,
> "Salvation belongs to our God who is seated on the throne, and to the Lamb!"
> And all the angels stood around the throne and around the elders and the living creatures, and they fell on their faces before the throne and worshiped God singing,
> "Amen! Blessing and glory and wisdom
> and thanksgiving and honor
> and power and might
> be to our God forever and ever! Amen."

Although there is not always agreement among commentators about whether the multitude was comprised of the martyrs who had survived the Great Tribulation, or was a symbolic reference to all who served God, the image is still clear. They were from every nation, all tribes and peoples and languages. There was no one who was not represented. No one was left out or left behind. All were of one accord and all maintained their cultures, their tribes, and their languages!

This is good news for us who believe in the possibility of being and building beloved community. It means that we are free to be authentically who God created us to be. All of us. We are free from the constraints of "othering," objectifying, or demonizing those who are visibly different from us. We are free to enter into the sacred space of experiencing the prodigal grace of oneness in God.

The Gospel of John quotes Jesus as saying,

> Whoever believes in me believes not in me but in him who sent me. And whoever sees me sees him who sent me. I have come as light into the world so that everyone who believes in me should not remain in the darkness. I do not judge anyone who hears my words and does not keep them, for I came not to judge the world, but to save the world."(John 12:47)

Jesus came to the house of Israel (Matt. 15:24). But he came for the world. The entire created order. All of creation. And he sent his disciples, not just to their own communities and families, not just to the people who shared customs and tribe and language— Jesus sent them into enemy territory into the territory of the "unclean," and indeed into all the world (Matt. 28:18-20).

Jesus' disciples were sent to teach, to preach, and to baptize in his name, his spirit, his nature, his love. Baptism in Jesus' name meant birth into a new reality. Paul tells us, "In the one spirit we were all baptized into one body—Jews or Greeks, slaves or free— and we were all made to drink of one spirit" (1 Cor. 12:13).

Christ, in whom we are one, goes with us. Beloved community will come. Opposers will be transformed into friends, goodwill will transform deep gloom into exuberant gladness, and the love of God in Christ Jesus will bring about miracles in the hearts of humans. Through our simple, consistent engagement with one another and the stories that are our lives, new beloved community will come, as surely as the dawn follows the night.

Bishop Linda Lee

Notes

1. "I Have a Dream," Speech, August 28, 1963, steps of the Lincoln Memorial, Washington, DC.

2. James, Perkinson, *White Theology: Outing Supremacy in Modernity* (New York: Palgrave Macmillan, 2004), 198. Quotation is from Franco Masciandaro, *Dante as Dramatist: The Myth of the Earthly Paradise and Tragic Vision in the Divine Comedy* (Philidelphia: Univerysity of Pennsylvania Press, 1991).

3. "Institutional racism is the intentional shaping and structuring of an institution so that it effectively serves and is accountable to one racial group and does not effectively serve nor is accountable to other racial groups (definition by Crossroads Ministry, which I [Barndt] have somewhat abbreviated and edited with their permission)." Joseph Barndt, *Understanding and Dismantling Racism: The Twenty-First Century Challenge to White America*, (Minneapolis: Fortress Press, 2007), 153.

4. Ibid.

5. John Wesley, *The Journal of John Wesley*, chapter 3, beginning on page 40.

6. Paul Lawrence Dunbar, "Representative American Negroes," *The Negro Problem*, Booker T. Washington (city: publisher, 1903), pages.

7. "Bitter Times," introduction (American Public Media, year).

8. Arturo Rosales, *Chicano: The History of the Mexican American Civil Rights Movement* (Houston: Arte Publico Press, 1997), 12.

9. Paul Kivel, *Uprooting Racism* (Gabriola, BC: New Society Publishers, 2011), 17, 19.

10. Ingrid Huygens, "From Colonization to Globalization: Continuities in Colonial 'Common Sense," *Critical Psychology* 2nd edition, Dennis Fox, Isaac Prilleltensky, and Stephanie Austin, eds. (Thousand Oaks, CA: Sage publications, Inc., 2009), 270.

11. Spring 2012 Intelligence Report, Southern Poverty Law Center.

12. Huygens, "From Colonization to Globalization," 268. 13. Michele Alexander, *The New Jim Crow*, Huff Post BOOKS, September, 17, 2012.

13. Michelle Alexander, *The New Jim Crow* (The New Press, 2012), p. 12.

For Further Reading

Council of Bishops of The United Methodist Church, 2011 Statement online at http://www.umc.org/atf/cf/%7Bdb6a45e4-c446-4248-82c8-e131b6424741%7D/BELOVED_COMMUNITY_STATEMENT.PDF

Inclusion: Making Room for Grace, Eric Law, Chalice Press, 2000.

White Theology, James W. Perkinson, Palgrave Macmillan, 2004.

CHAPTER ONE

Tiospaye, Brothers and Sisters, Listen Carefully

Ray Buckley

My house is in Alaska, near the Matanuska River.

My home is the Paha Sapa (Black Hills), across the Northwest, to the great Pacific rainforest of British Columbia and Alaska. I have known it intimately and its flow of seasons, since I was a child. It is part of my bones. My home is the salmon, the rain, the trees, the rocks, and the bones of those I have never known, and those I have loved. When the dawn comes, I sing.

My church home is the Clinton Indian United Methodist Church, St. John United Methodist Church, and a gathering of Native men who meet to eat, laugh, study the Bible, and pray with one another.

If you are half-Native, you will be compelled at some time in your life to make a choice. You will be proud of all that you are and embrace with open arms that which God has created. But you will have to make a choice. To not choose is to choose.

In a traditional setting, I would stand in front of you so that you were able to see my face and my person. I would dress to honor and respect you, but choose not to be more than you are able to be. I would say to you, "I'm standing with you. See, there is nothing between you and me." I am choosing that there is nothing between you and me. In this moment, for this day, we will call each other, Standing-with-Nothing-Between.

One begins with a sense of their-own-Beloved-ness.[1] Not perfection or even rightness. Beloved-ness. Embraced by the One, which having all, knowing all, chooses to love you. The oil from your hands. The texture of your hair. The sound of your voice in your language. Without that sense of beloved-ness, one sees others through fear, envy, or self-contempt.

Sweet Honey in the Rock, a profound vocal ensemble of African American women sings a song that echoes through the spirit: "There Were No Mirrors in My Nana's House" (Ysaye/Marie Barnwell; copyright 1992). It sings of finding your self-image not through a reflection in glass but through the mirror of a grand-mother's eyes. Beloved-ness.

The heart of community is *recognizing* and *needing* the beloved-ness of one another and ourselves. It is beginning to see one another, individuals and cultures, through the eyes of God. Stealing the beloved-ness of another is the heart of self-importance.

Many times, a person will embrace me or take my hands, and say, "I am so sorry for what has been done to your people." I so often say, "I am sorry for what has been done to yours." It is a simple, truthful, statement. The gospel compels us to say more, "I am so sorry for what has been done to you." I am sorry for what has been done to the beloved-ness of the Standing-before-me-person-with-nothing-between.

I once asked my father, who was part of a sister Wesleyan denomination, if one could be a Christian and hate others. He said, "Yes." There was a moment of silence. "But not for long. God will always ask you to love Another."

When I choose to move beyond self-interest and preservation into relationship, I am choosing to participate in what is unfamiliar to me but essential to the nature of God. If I don't, I choose not to open myself to God, and that is the beginning of profound loneliness.

To permit my spirit to live in superiority is to be fractured in my spirit. It is to deny God the opportunity to do something significant for me through the life of another. It is an antithesis of the holiness, wholeness, which God intends for me.

The Wisdom of a People

One of the seven sacred rites of the Lakota is the *Making of Relatives*. At its core is the identity of a people who believe that extending familial relationship to others is a sacred responsibility.

It is not done recklessly or carelessly, and the ceremony is one of great significance to the people. Once entered into, the one adopted is always referred to by relationship (father, mother, brother, sister). He or she is introduced to others by relationship (She is my grandmother), without any other qualifiers, for there are none. As in many tribes, a Lakota person, by spiritual responsibility, makes family.

The responsibility of *Making of Relatives* is significant. One assumes the care of, the social responsibilities for, and the love of the one(s) whom they have adopted. Thereafter, they are truly related. It is not a, "We are like sisters," relationship, but rather a "We are sisters." From then on, all of the tribe(s) will introduce the two of you (or more) as sisters (or grandfather, grandmother, father, mother, brother).

The effect is far reaching to the smallest detail. In most Native cultures, stories and songs belong to individuals or families. Social etiquette requires that you do not sing the song of another, or tell the story of another. Those songs and stories may be given by a family to another, so that they also may share them in the appropriate setting. When you have been adopted you are included in the family songs at tribal events. You are given the right to sing the songs and tell the stories in the correct cultural context. You have become part of the history of a person and his or her family. When there is a birth, you celebrate with the family. When there is a death, you mourn with the family, all the while celebrating, singing, mourning, and telling the stories of the family in which you were born, and those they have adopted.

This circle expands to the community, *tiospaye*, or extended family, those persons of love and importance, all known as grandparents, aunties, uncles, and cousins, from numerous places. The language is such that simple greetings cannot be said without finding a way to describe relationship.

Mitaque oyasin, "all my relations," speaks to the related-ness of all which is created. In a deeply profound way, all creation responds to change in relationship. There is a theological physics to relationship. In a Christian understanding, we might say that Easter moved Creation.

Most Native languages utilize the passive voice, and those who speak English as a second language, speak and write in the passive voice. It is not a lack of English education that causes us to choose the passive voice, but our understanding of who we are among others and the world around us. We choose to move beyond editorial norms to speak English in a manner that does not assert ourselves over others.

To remove one's language or choice of "voice" is to remove the person's understanding of the world and how he or she relates to it. It also prevents that worldview, through language, from edifying the faith community.

A Native child in a traditional community learns that one never puts oneself forward. You do not speak of yourself or your accomplishments except in well-defined settings. You do not brag. Humility and community are twin sisters. A Native child in a traditional community seldom raises a hand in a classroom. One does not compete for attention but rather helps others succeed. Making eye contact for long periods of time is considered rude, as is raising your voice. One waits to share an opinion until others have spoken. Once an elder speaks, one does not disagree in public. We are part of a People, and the protocols of our cultures keep our beliefs alive.

All participation in ritual is based on humility. A person who is not humble is not respected in the community. Encouraging or expecting persons to act in a way that is not humble is to encourage them to violate their culture. Sharing, serving, and lifting others up are the ways we are taught to live.

Our deepest cultural roots, our stories of creation and emergence, speak in more personal ways than the creation of the whole world. They speak to us of how we emerged as a people(s). They speak to us of why we are a part of this land, in this place, in this creation, and why we are unique. We continually come back to our stories of origin to remind us of who we are. Our ability to find reference to our beginnings and culture enables us to live with credibility and respectfulness in the broader world.

Our understanding of human-being-ness, vastly distinct from *humanism*, is that we are created beings, part of other created beings. Our names for ourselves, in our languages, most often mean *human beings*, or *people*. There is no religious action that is not based in relationship. In truth, in many Native understandings of life, there is no function of life that is not based in relationship. Holiness for many Native peoples is living in relationship: living in a *right* or *good way*. Not in docile agreeability, but in active, engaged relationship. The antitheses of holy living are those choices that destroy healthy, sacred relationship. Persons who choose to do so chip away at their human-being-ness, their created-purpose-ness, and need to be restored. We are restored into relationship, for the purpose of relationship. We are in community.

My internal "house," my waking-up-place, my lying-down-place, my Home, is my understanding of community.

When the historic, institutional church, taught us that we could not be truly Native and Christian, we directed our shame inward. We questioned our own Beloved-ness. We questioned our Home.

In Lakota, the word commonly associated with "white people," *wasicu(n)*, has nothing to do with skin color. When used as a race description, it is rather an historical reference to how the first-encounter-experience impacted The People. It literally means, "fat stealers," or "stealers of the fat."

To survive, human beings need protein, but also fat. So critical was fat for the survival of Native people, that it was never wasted. Many game proteins were so lean that having meat was not enough. An offering of fat to a visitor was a gift of value.

The importance of that first encounter was that Anglo people came into the village at night and stole all of the fat. They literally stole the means of survival, the ability of a people to survive the winter. The descriptive word for white people does not refer to their light skin color, but to how they impacted the survival of a group of people. In the Lakota language, they became those that stole the ability to survive.

There is a sad irony. Those who stole the fat were also seeking to survive. It was our custom to share, but they didn't give us the chance to tell them.

The effect of racism prohibits the ability of a people to flourish or prosper in a spiritual, cultural, and economic reality. Tolerance allows the continuance, survival, and presence of a people, but just barely. Tolerance is racism on hold.

Within the church, we have allowed for the *tolerated maintenance* of marginalized communities, and we truly desire their presence, because we value the importance of diversity. However, marginal-ized communities within the church always exist at the discretion of the church. Self-protection (economic, structural, or theological) allows the church, allows us, to exercise that discretion. That has always been the problem with "home missions" (wherever home is). That which is the closest to us is the least likely to be idealized and may become annoying or threatening. It is what turns up in our own yard that causes us to be fearful.

The beautiful Tlingit culture of southeast Alaska and British Columbia is divided into two distinct familial groups, called moieties: Raven and Eagle. Within each moiety, inherited from one's mother, are clans associated with either the Raven or Eagle.

Disputes between clans, which at one time had been settled by violence, were settled by sending volunteer captives (known as deer) to the clan house of the offended party. The deer would be fed, treated well, and allowed to live in the home of their enemy until an appropriate time had passed. The deer would then be returned home, and the conflict was ended. It was a cultural tool to restore peace.

One day, deer arrived at the clan house of the offended party. They were received well, fed well, treated with respect, and then killed. The protocol had been broken, never returning. We had killed the deer and could no longer be politely civil.

Slavery and Sand Creek

Slavery in the Americas began with Native people. In many places, the church was complicit with those who came to take possession. By the time John Wesley arrived in Georgia, the English had already enslaved whole populations of tribes to the point of extinction. While smaller bands and tribes disappeared, larger tribes were significantly affected. In particular, the Choctaw people were captured with the aid of the Creeks, and sold into slavery in the Caribbean and Europe. Because of the innate connection between Anglicanism and the national interests of England, in the American southeast, Native people often suffered under *expansionistic evangelism.* Expansionistic evangelism would characterize much of Native ministry. The historical church has never been able to escape the temptation of power, and the ability to use it. It has often been, and often found, willing partners.

Until the Emancipation Proclamation, in California, it was legal to indenture a Native person for sixteen years for a price of $2.

Young women and girls sold into slavery brought the highest prices; $300 for a child around ten years of age. Native people in the southern regions of the state were sold as agricultural slaves. In 1848, at the time of the gold rush, estimates of the population of Native people in California were close to 150,000. Thirty years later, it was close to 30,000.

Pre-Columbian estimates of Native populations are in the millions. In 1900, there were about 250,000 Native souls remaining in the United States.

Tiospaye, my brothers and sisters, listen carefully. Native children, as young as five years old, were removed from their homes and raised in institutional boarding schools. There they were taught to read the Bible. If they spoke in their tribal languages, they were beaten. Their hair was cut off, and they were made to wear military-style uniforms. They were not raised by mothers and fathers or grandparents. They were raised in dormitories by boarding school staff. There is not a Native family in the United States or Canada that has not been touched by the boarding-school experience. The now famous motto of one of the largest boarding schools says simply, "Kill the Indian. Save the child."

Most often, boarding schools were operated by mainline denominations, including both The Methodist Episcopal Church, and The Methodist Episcopal Church South. Documentable physical, sexual, and mental abuse of children in boarding schools and remote tribal communities by church employees is profound. Currentcourt cases in the United States and Canada number in the thousands.

National laws were passed making it illegal to teach Native children in their own languages. Until the 1970s, Native children could be removed from their homes without the consent of their parents. Church institutions served as the largest purveyors of Native children, adopting them to families on either side of the U.S. and Canadian border and often destroying the records.

The effort to eliminate the *Making of Relatives* and the extended family resulted in the breaking up and dispersing of nuclear families. Grandparents were sent to one part of the country; parents and children to another. Many spiritual leaders, homosexual persons, the elderly, persons with disabilities, and the uniquely gifted; all who had been welcomed, protected, and included in tribal communities, became outcasts under the new systems. In the new "community" being taught to our children, those persons from whom the Creator had intended for us to learn new spiritual things, were isolated.

Certainly, one of the effects of false-community is the mistaken belief that I need to transform others into myself. Once I have scrubbed *Them*, ironed *Them*, and educated *Them* into *My* image, *I* remind *Them* that they are not *Me*. Nor did I ever expect *Them* to be.

In 1862, John Chivington, clergy and former presiding elder (equivalent of district superintendent) of the Rocky Mountain Conference of The Methodist Episcopal Church in the Denver area, was listed in *The Rocky Mountain News*. He and Territorial Governor John Evans were listed as two of five members of the board of trustees for the formation of a new Methodist Episcopal congregation in Denver. The reverend Chivington and Governor Evans had been the key figures in the formation of Denver Seminary, a Methodist Episcopal institution.

In 1864, bands of Cheyenne and Arapahoe gathered on the plains of Colorado at Sand Creek. Under a white flag of peace and an American flag, the Cheyenne and Arapaho, had been promised and had every expectation of safety. At dawn, on November 29, against the advice of other officers, Colonel Chivington engaged his soldiers at the peaceful encampment. The massacre was brutal. Women and children fled and were chased on horseback until they were shot or bayoneted. Some literally were followed for miles. When the carnage was over, Native men, women, and children were scalped and mutilated.

In the streets of Denver, Colonel Chivington and his men were welcomed as heroes. Some wore the sexual organs of Native women on their hats as souvenirs. Scalps and other body parts of the Cheyenne and Arapaho hung from saddles. Across the stage of a Denver theater, ropes were stretched displaying the bloodied and stinking pieces of humanity, while citizens of Denver strolled through to see them. Some of the human skin and organs were tanned and used as book covers. Some was used for Bibles.

There are hundreds of events in which those affiliated with Methodism and the predecessor institutions that formed The United Methodist Church knowingly participated in brutal racial acts and caused the death of Native people. Annual conferences not only supported but assisted in the forced removal of the

Cherokee, Chickasaw, Choctaw, Creek, and Seminole from the Southeast to Indian Territory, while Native Methodists carried pieces of their churches with them as they walked to Oklahoma.

The importance of Sand Creek is not that it stands out above the other histories. There are Native people in Methodist churches who have known living survivors of Sand Creek, Wounded Knee, the murders of the Osage, and too many to count. There are those who were born in prison during the decades-long imprisonment of the Fort Sill Apache. There are those who were beaten for singing their Native hymns, and those of us who remember well the signs that said "No Indians or dogs allowed." What stands out about Sand Creek is that it is *one* of many places to begin healing. Not the healing of Native people. The healing of the church.

Our healing is the beginning of Beloved Community. Healing begins when we leave the deer behind and seek one another.

The simple truth and complex problem for The United Methodist Church is that within our institutions are collections that are inappropriate for anything connected with the liberation of the Gospel. In recent years, some institutions have quietly transferred Native relics to non-Native institutions, without consultation with the church or Native communities. There are sacred objects over which mourning needs to take place. These are not just memorabilia of a different time and place. They cannot simply be sent elsewhere. They must be treated in a sacred manner dictated by the people to whom they belong. In our inability or unwillingness to deal with their presence, we perpetuate our own histories as well as the loss of indigenous people. We do not talk about it, while Native people have a "deep knowing."

Within our traditional cultures, what has been taken forcibly from another becomes the spiritual responsibility of the one who took it (and all of their descendants). If something is irresponsibly lost, the spiritual responsibility still exists until a sacred action is taken.

It is not true that we can repent only for what we have done. Among Native people, there is no distinction between Methodists, Catholics, Presbyterians, and others. As Native United Methodists, we wear the history of Christianity around our shoulders every time we walk into a tribal community. Along with the "Gospel of Jesus Christ," which we willingly wear, we also *carry the shame of the church. Our church.* In the eyes of the abused, atrocities committed in the name of Christ are born by all who carry the name, including Christ.

All formal acts of repentance by denominations have led to further division and pain among Native populations. Inevitably, churches as institutions, and those serving as their representatives, will act only as far as their best interest. Beyond that, they must either discredit themselves, or Native people, as individuals or groups.

Tisospaye, brothers and sisters, listen carefully. We have not yet mourned for what we do to each other. We have not yet offered to carry each other's crosses. I am not given the luxury of placing myself or my people in competition with those who are suffering or have suffered. As a Christian, and a Native person, I am compelled by the love of God to help carry the burdens of a farmer in Missouri or a baker in the Ukraine. I am *compelled.* Because, among all peoples of the world, historical trauma is a preface to the trauma of the future, I am compelled to help carry the burdens of others continually. Such is the grace of Beloved Community.

By the grace of God, we are told; our sins are forgiven and held no longer against us. The confusion for those we wound is that they still see our faces, can still call us by name, and still get up in the morning with an altered life for which we are responsible. They wonder, "What kind of religion, what kind of God, allows cavalier abuse, committed and forgotten, leaving the multi-generational wounded in the wake?"

C. S. Lewis writes,

> It may be that salvation consists not in the canceling of these eternal moments but in the perfected humility that bears the shame forever, rejoicing in the occasion which it furnished to God's compassion and glad that it should be common knowledge to the universe.[2]

Might it be so that in Beloved Community we are called to not cover the sin but to grasp it with both hands, acknowledging that our weakness has been the occasion of God's strength in creating something new?

False community within the church so impacts the sharing of the Gospel, that the Gospel itself is shamed in the eyes of the wounded.

What I do to others, I do to the person of God. Fundamentally. Literally.

Several years ago, a young man I did not know called my office. He was calling in a non-official way, about an idea he had. On reservations across the United States, tribal colleges were doing remarkable work in enabling reservation young people to attend college at home, receiving an education in culturally and linguistically affirming ways. Their results were measurable and remarkable. However, tribal colleges were in desperate need of funding, and even though enrollment costs were low for tribal members, many young people did not have access to money for college. He had heard of the Native American Ministries Sunday Offering of The United Methodist Church. He said simply, "I have an idea. Would you folks consider using the offering to help talented, at-risk young people go to college?" He paused for a moment. "Imagine, instead of seeing the face of one United Methodist seminary student, you could literally see the faces of hundreds of Native young people. Our kids could develop a relationship with your churches, and you could develop a relationship with our people and tribal colleges." For a moment,

for a moment, there was this feeling of a simple idea, so related to Native culture and people.

The World in Which We Live

Native people as a whole have one of the highest rates of suicide in the world. Native youth have the highest rate in the world.

Native women are ten times more likely to be murdered than the national average. In 2011, the Indian Law Resource Center documents that one out of three will be raped; three out of five will be sexually assaulted. Amnesty International reports that in addition to the violence of rape, Native women are more likely to suffer additional brutal violence when raped. The U.S. Department of Justice reports that in 88 percent of cases of rape and aggressive violence against Native women, the perpetrators are non-Native.

Seventy percent of the violence experienced by Native people as a whole is committed by persons of a different race.

Violent crimes committed against Native people by non-Native people increases yearly.

Tiospaye, brothers and sisters. Listen carefully. Today, at this moment in time, active racism allows Native women to be seen as reasonable and acceptable *objects* to be humiliated even to the point of death. Active and increasing racism allows Native people as a whole to be seen as socially acceptable targets of violence.

Every year, the Alaska Federation of Natives brings tribal representatives from over two hundred tribes to meet in either Anchorage or Fairbanks. Native women are escorted from meetings to their hotels to protect them from violence.

A profound expression of racism is to intentionally remove any sense of beloved-ness held by another, by violating the body and spirit.

Listening to People with Beards

An Athabascan elder once said, "Our people have been taught and come to believe that only men with beards can teach them to be holy." Oh, dear God.

False community within the church is the continuing belief that marginalized groups are incapable of effectively determining their future.

Tiospaye, my brothers and sisters, listen carefully. Today, when regions of our church look at ministry among Native people, we look to "men with beards," non-Native authorities, for solutions.

In the late 1800s through the middle of the last century, mainline denominations were given "religious rights" to Native tribes. Tribes that had been Episcopal became Lutheran, or Baptist, or Methodist. People who had been Presbyterian became Catholic. They were not given a choice. Though the Comity Agreements no longer exist, in the Christian community, they are still honored. Within portions of our Methodist system, decisions are made regarding Native people or communities, only with the permission and collegial agreement of other denominations. Native people become a possession of denominations to be agreed upon. History repeats itself.

More than a half century before The United Methodist Church ordained women, many of our sister Wesleyan denominations ordained women. The Wesleyan Church was founded around the issue of eliminating slavery, while we debated it. Sister denominations saw their *identity* in ministry to the poor.

Native boarding schools, covert removal and adoption of Native children, the reservation system, forced registration of Native people, Comity Agreements, and many other devastating policies originated with Christian groups who believed that it was in the "best interest" of Native people to make decisions for them. We make decisions for them because we believe that they are fundamentally incapable of choosing correctly.

False community is the belief that exercising power over another is permissible, and justifiable, if I perceive that they are incapable of making right decisions.

Vine Deloria, Jr., in *Singing for a Spirit: A Portrait of the Dakota Sioux* (Clear Light, Santa Fe NM, 1999), speaks of the role of his family in the Episcopal evangelization of Dakota tribal bands. Among the small group of Native men chosen for the ministry was Phillip Joseph Deloria, a highly successful pastor in the Sioux communities. Each year, at the annual camp meeting along the Niobrara River, about 20,000 Lakota/Dakota Christians gathered for a time of worship, prayer, community, and social interaction. Hymns were sung in Dakota. Preaching was in Dakota. Tipis were set up as far as the eye could see. Episcopal organizations sent representatives to Niobrara and reported to church bodies back east.

By the time I was a child, the Native Christians who gathered at Niobrara would scarcely reach 2,000 in attendance, with non-Native people setting up folding chairs and bringing boxed lunches to "watch the Indians."

Deloria speaks of the decline of Episcopal work among the Dakota as being directly related to the refusal to place Native clergy in leadership positions in Native ministry, even among their own people. In the early years of ministry effort, a handful of Native men were displayed around the church at church events, until one by one they became disheartened.

The Native reality is painful, costly, and not curiously, foreign. It is that foreignness that confuses us about Native cultures and also compels us to seek acquiescence of Native cultures into western religious thought and practices.

Father Michael Oleksa, a non-Native Russian Orthodox priest, Russian Orthodox apologist, scholar, and student of Native cultures, refers to Native ways of thinking, as "Another culture, another world." There is probably not a more accurate and succinct way of expressing the idea. Native people think and act, grounded in a culture often unfamiliar to the world in which they live. Another culture, another world.

Within The United Methodist Church are people groups around the world, whose cultures, values, and worldviews are different from the American church, and from one another. Sometimes in order to participate in our denomination, they are required to come to the table acting, speaking, and behaving differently than they believe. It is like thinking in one language and using a dictionary to help you speak in another. *Tiospaye*, my brothers and sisters, listen carefully. Sometimes the political process of the church exploits the cultures of our peoples for our own gain, while we overlook our need for their presence in the continual revitalization of the church.

The Poor You Have with You

Brothers and sisters, within a short period of time, most of the members of The United Methodist Church will be poor by Western standards and worshiping in small membership churches.

Native people as a whole represent the poorest population in the Western Hemisphere, except the nation of Haiti.

The majority of United Methodist Native clergy are literally ordained into poverty.

We are reminded that coal miners would take a caged canary into the mines with them. The canary would be the first indicator of a lack of oxygen.

It is widely accepted by those who study Native-Church relations that The Oklahoma Indian Missionary Conference of The United Methodist Church is one of the vital "canaries" of indigenous Christianity. Its presence is strategic for several unique factors. Its membership and local ministries represent the largest collective of diverse, active Native cultures, languages, and Native-Christian experience(s) in the Wesleyan movement. Its varied Native-Christian expressions and theologies are some of the purest forms of tribulation and liberation worship/thought in Wesleyanism.

In the early part of the last century, when the historical Indian Mission was dissolved against the wishes of Indian churches, one half of the Native membership left the denomination and did not return.

For Native people, as with other people groups, community is not synonymous with assimilation. We already exist as part of the church, and we exist as distinct, viable cultures within the church. We bear testimony to the presence of the Spirit of God among our unique peoples. The Spirit of God changes us when we encounter the Spirit of God in others. We become the unborn John the Baptist, leaping within the womb of his mother Elizabeth when encountering the unborn Christ.

Like her sister, The Red Bird Missionary Conference, The Oklahoma Indian Missionary Conference confirms the Wesleyan commitment to the poor and marginalized.

History has shown us that from the poor and marginalized will emerge the theologies and graces to refresh the future church. The poor are not just the ministry of the church; they are the heart of Beloved Community.

The Poor Have Received the Gospel

Tiospaye, my brothers and sisters, listen carefully.

We often speak of the mission period of the church among Native and indigenous people as if it were in the past. As an outward movement of the evangelistic effort of Methodism, the church has been in mission with Native people for over two hundred years. We are simply in the beginning moments of the *inward* movement of allowing Native people to impact the Body of Christ. The inward movement of mission is when the work of God among global peoples flows into the thought process and spiritual practice of the church to such a degree, that the church becomes the image of the Spirit of God in action. Mission is circular.

When the words *mission* or *missionary* are used around Native people in traditional communities, there is a measurable stress response, even among children.

We need to remind ourselves that persons in marginalized communities, whether in developing countries or economic powers, pay extraordinary prices for becoming disciples of Jesus Christ.

Among a small number of U.S. tribes, Native people may lose their ability to inherit allocated reservation land if they become Christian. Native people in Alaska, British Columbia, and Siberia are still excommunicated from the Russian Orthodox Church if they become United Methodist. The effect is to be shunned. It is similar throughout the global church. We do not come to the church carrying a Bible; we come to the church carrying our lives.

In the late 1800s through the middle 1900s, mainline Christian denominations sent missionaries to Native villages, remote communities, and rural reservations. We built church buildings and began worshiping communities that became vital to Native people. When we could no longer provide clergy in those settings, either by lack of available appointees or funding, we kept claim to the ministries and properties but no longer served them, except periodically. Sometimes not at all.

Across Alaska, Canada, and the contiguous United States are Native villages and communities with empty church buildings. Sometimes a clergy person is present once or twice a year. Sometimes not at all. In some cases, remnants of congregations are led by laypersons. There is a correlation between the number of suicides in a community and the lack of either traditional or Christian spiritual leaders.

We baptized believers, both as a statement of faith and into the church. We served the Eucharist as a physical expression of the spiritual act of remembering the death and resurrection of Jesus. And then we left. For decades, some Native communities have not had a baptism or the opportunity to celebrate Communion. For decades.

There is a profound element of racism in our inability to provide the sacraments to marginalized communities. It is an issue for the whole church. It is however, an issue that disproportionately affects the poor and at-risk populations around the world.

The inability to access the sacraments is an inability to participate fully in Beloved Community.

A few years ago, Native Christian leaders from several mainline denominations gathered in Laramie, Wyoming to pray and talk about the sacraments. The conclusion of the Laramie Agreement was that the issue of being "fully connected" to the experience of the Christian faith was so significant that in the continual absence of pastoral care, our elders would baptize and serve the Eucharist. When the *traditions* of the church prohibit or prevent acts of grace within the church, we cease to be community and become protectors and benefactors.

All sacraments are relational. Sacraments are gifts of God for the creation and continuance of relationship, and are the fundamental right of adoption to every believer.

Tiospaye, my brothers and sisters, listen carefully. In the absence of active congregations with pastoral leadership, independent ministries are experiencing growth in accessible villages and reservations, often bringing with them a return to theologies that minimize the role of women and identify Native cultures as sinful.

The poor have received the gospel but are unable to keep it, practice it, or regularly engage in the intimacies of community.

Killing the Church's Indian

Author Fergus M. Bordewich wrote an insightful look into Native communities, issues, and governmental relationships entitled, *Killing the White Man's Indian* (Anchor Books, 1996).

Within the church, our perception of others can create false reality (good or bad), leading to unrealistic expectations of response. Among Native people our perception of what the church wants us to be can become a false identity: The *church's Indian*. The church's Indian will morph into the expectations of the institution, often at the expense of the Native experience.

We often replace engagement with Native communities, with Native-like representation in the church structure. It is easier to *create icons* of individual Native people than to struggle with the realities of Native communities. An annual conference located within a region with one of the largest percentages of Native people has made it a practice to appoint one single Native person at a time to as many conference, jurisdictional, and general offices as possible. One at a time.

As Native people, we are complicit in creating icons. Many young, seminary graduates with little experience seek recognition within the church on the basis of their Native identity. When that doesn't come, or doesn't come to the degree they expect, they become angry and disillusioned with the church. The desire to become the next "icon" in The United Methodist Church creates competitiveness. In the process, an essential element of the Native experience is lost: humility and the lifting up of others.

Native people come in all colors and sizes. I am biracial. My skin is not brown. I was attending a church Native event with an African American elder. She kindly asked, "What have you done with all of the brown people?" It is a heart-rending question of community. Has what we (as Native people) have made of Native community in the church alienated the core of our people, until those most identifiable with tribal communities seek community elsewhere? Have we become so lost and prideful in being the church's Indians that we can neither accurately inform the community of the church nor interest our people?

Is it permissible to say that the political process of our church, so familiar in the United States, is seen as brutal and nonspiritual in many world cultures? In the Beloved Community, what we export by example is as much a spiritual question as what we import and internalize.

The work of the people of God is not just *making* disciples of Jesus Christ, but *being* disciples of Jesus Christ for the transformation of the world. We are to intentionally break down the walls, remove the coins from our own eyes, see the Other as part of ourselves, and live.

My race, when used for self-aggrandizement and competitiveness becomes racism. Beloved Community begins with my humility.

Within our denomination, indigenous cultures around the world sing Christmas carols during Advent, Christmas, Epiphany, and Ordinary Time. In desperately poor communities, the hymns we have written in our languages are sung as gifts to each other, when the only other gifts we may receive will be the sharing of food. Two years ago, the tribal hymnbooks were removed from a northern Midwestern Native church to prevent the elders from singing Christmas hymns during Advent. In an act of incarnational birth control, a Western church tradition was used to try and silence the gifts another culture was offering to God and the world.

Native people from tribal communities often do not recognize the worship or cultural expressions identified as Native within the church, because they have been created or altered for the church.

Recently, with a small group of Native people, we were asked to walk in circles around a communion table, burning sage, and beating a drum. None of us had experienced anything like it before. It was not part of our tribal or church experiences. It had been conceived by a worship leader as something "Native American." We do not invent the cultures of our people. Instead, when the time came, we sang a simple hymn.

The *Beauty Way* is a Dine (Navajo) ceremony lasting several days. It reflects the core of Dine belief, cosmology, theology, and identity. Because of its profound beauty, we have taken phrases from the Beauty Way ceremony and incorporated them into Christian worship.

The Creek hymn "Heleluyan" is begun by a lead singer. When sung traditionally, before the chorus is completed, the leader is already beginning the verse, so that the singing never stops. In our hymnal we removed the verses and altered the style of the song to make it passable for non-Native singers. Doing so, we lost the circular nature of the hymn.

We have taken Native prayers and pieces of ancient ceremonies and adapted them for Christian worship. The church has taken sweetgrass, cedar, sage, pipe, and water ceremonies, traditional stories, and songs for its own use. We have taken them out of context and away from where they belong, and used them for our own purpose, while at the same time condemning Native traditional beliefs and practices. We have taken sacred stories and reduced them to three minute news spots. Prayers and songs that were believed to renew the earth, now serve to fill the bulletin on Native American Ministries Sunday.

When we appropriate Native spiritual and cultural elements (or other world cultures) for our own use, altering their context and purposes, the church engages in cultural theft. However well intentioned, cultural theft contributes to cultural genocide. The intent and relational impact of spiritual practices are eroded.

Tiospaye, my brothers and sisters. Listen carefully. What God has given a people for their spiritual welfare and survival is intrinsic to their identity. Inside the church, neither Native nor non-Native persons, no individual, has the right to give away or appropriate the inheritance of a people.

Is it conceivable that in our attempt to be diverse, we ask the peoples of the world to write in English, perpetuating the loss of language and culture in tribal communities worldwide? Who will write for the Lakota? Who will write for the Salish or Cree? Who will write in the language in which The People (any people) think and pray? Who will write songs, vocables, and prayers that can never be translated in other languages and posted to websites because the images are so personal to a people?

Is not Beloved Community the weaving of the testimony of the saints of God, by God? Not the cacophony of the Tower of Babel, but the day of Pentecost, when all heard in their own languages. We are called to be the people that God made us, until the songs from which angels fold their wings infuse the church, and the church says, "Yes."

This Community of the Beloved

Several years ago, as The United Methodist Church prepared for an advertising campaign and training for welcoming respondents, pastors within a region of the United States with a large population of Native persons were asked, "If Native people responded to advertising campaigns, visited your church, would they be welcomed as part of your congregation?" The overwhelming, apologetic response was a truthful, no. Some responded that "professional" Native persons might be welcome.

We, the community of the church, weren't quite prepared for people whose culture made them reluctant to share their names and contact information on a first visit. We weren't quite prepared for families who wouldn't conceive of sending their children to a separate service, and were reluctant to make eye contact. We were confused when they rested their hands in ours instead of gripping them. We were confused because they lived in our neighborhood.

In a jurisdictional meeting examining projected ministry needs across a region with large Native populations, two specific groups were omitted: Native people, and large populations of migrant workers. The response was simply, "We listed only those groups in which we had an interest in ministry."

We were confused as Native people, when an elderly white couple brought their folding chairs and sat in the pow-wow circle along with the rest of us.

What will we do as community if folks not only visit, but decide to stay? By the grace of God, our community will change.

There is a church near the New Mexico border that is largely made up of ranching families. The roads to the church are slick with red mud during rain, and when it is dry, everything is covered in red dust. Many years the church had no pastor, the congregation meeting anyway. Attendance was usually small, depending on the time of year. I arrived to speak on a Sunday morning and saw a simple white building surrounded by close-cropped grass. The grass was full of pick-up trucks. The young pastor was a seminary student who had been a welder by trade.

There was no longer a front door; it and a portion of the wall had been replaced by a large sliding door that one would use on a barn. The whole back of the building was open to the community. The pulpit had been replaced by a welded art lectern fashioned from old ranching equipment. The communion table, refined and stately, had been remade from fencepost. The pulpit furniture was redesigned farm equipment, and the baptismal was a welded basin and water pump. I walked into a sanctuary of beautiful art and proud parishioners. I walked into a church were a young pastor and his family had listened to the voices and needs of his congregation and created worship from the joys and hardships of their hands. This was a building that told a story of years gone by, and a culture still in continuance. Beloved Community

The descendants of the Cheyenne and Arapaho pray over the ground where the massacre occurred. Each year, runners hallow the earth itself by running over the killing field and the paths of flight. For days, some will fast, all pray, others run, in the hopes of restoring the earth and healing the memory.

Conference superintendent of the Oklahoma Indian Missionary Conference, David Wilson, drove by a closed church building on the Cheyenne-Arapahoe Reservation. There was a small group of children holding worship on the concrete pad in front of the locked door. Stopping, he asked them if they were there every Sunday. They said, "Yes." They came when there was sadness. They came to the locked church when they were in trouble. That day, adult volunteers came and have been there ever since. Beloved Community.

Christians in Nazi death camps would create a form of communion. Before partaking, they would ask each other, "Have I done something to you for which I need to ask forgiveness?" Having reconciled themselves to each other, they would partake of the Lord's Table. Beloved Community.

Belgian Catholic priest, the late Father Louis Evele, phrased it graphically:

> No one feeds on Christ's flesh
> and no one's a naturalized citizen of heaven
> until,
>   along with the host,
> he can swallow all his neighbors.[3]

Hear the words of our Lord, as remembered by our brother, John, in his writing:

"Let me give you a new command: Love one another. In the same way I loved you, you love one another. This is how everyone will recognize that you are my disciples—when they see the love you have for each other." (John 13:34; *The Message*)

Loving God is what we expect. Loving our neighbors is more than an extraneous thought. It is a new commandment, given a new order by Jesus. Loving God and loving our neighbor is relationship. I do not choose my neighbors. I am compelled to love them. And the way that others recognize that I am a disciple of Jesus Christ is the manner in which I love others.

Singing to a new dawn. There is the beginning of Beloved Community in the church and the world where the church lives and breathes: We are to love God completely, and our neighbor as ourselves.

The idea of Beloved Community is rich and inspiring. Beyond our period of contemplation, beyond the retreat and reflection, Beloved Community requires the willingness to not only leave our door open but to walk into darkened passages where we cannot see more than a few feet. To go where we have not been, but God is.

Beloved Community is not passive. It is to encounter and engage. It is to make serious mistakes regularly. It is to expect and experience failure. Beloved Community is also to know that once you take the step, you cannot go back to where you were before.

There is beauty in the simple words of Acts 1:14:

They agreed they were in this for good, completely together in prayer, the women included. Also Jesus' mother and his brothers. (*The Message*)

They agreed that they were in this for good. They agree that they—that they—were in this for good.

A clergy friend of mine significantly struggled with the practice of giving an invitation or "altar call" in some denominations. Her parishioners often told her that one of their most meaningful experiences came during the celebration of the Eucharist. The celebrant speaks the words to the gathered congregation, "In the name of Christ you are forgiven." The congregation speaks the words to the celebrant, "In the name of Christ *you* are forgiven."

In the gift of the confessional, the penitent brings his or her sins to the community of heaven and the church, through the priests. In those private moments, the priest offers acts of penance, not as a requirement of grace, but as restoration to the community. In a simpler tradition, those seeking grace walk to the front of the church, and the community comes to surround them with prayer. In all of our ways, we seek not only the grace of God but restoration to Beloved Community.

The meaningful moment for my friend's parishioners' was hearing the voice of the community speak the grace of God. It is one thing to know that you are forgiven. It is a gift of grace to hear it spoken to you by those around you. It is also a gift of grace to speak it to someone else.

"My dear friends, if God loves us like this, we certainly ought to love each other. No one has seen God, ever. But if we love one another, God dwells deeply within us, and his love becomes complete in us—perfect love!" (1 John 4:11-12; *The Message*)

We have agreed that we are in this for good, completely together in prayer. Completely together in prayer.

The Apostle Peter, having been sent to the house of Cornelius by the Holy Spirit in Acts 10, is given a vision at noon. In the vision, a blanket is lowered with all kind of unclean animals on it. The message is clear. Kill and eat. Three times the blanket is lowered, and each time the message is the same. Kill and eat. In Peter's tradition he cannot eat or touch anything unclean. He refuses. The message from the Holy Spirit is simple, "If God says it's okay, it's okay." A short while later, Peter would proclaim to Gentile believers, "God doesn't play favorites."

We have agreed that we are in this for good, completely together in prayer. If God says someone or something is okay, it's okay. God doesn't play favorites. Beloved Community.

It is a traditional setting. I am standing in front of you so that you are able to see my face and my person. I dressed to honor and respect you, but choose not to be more than you are able to be. I say to you, "I'm standing with you. See, there is nothing between you and me." I am choosing that there is nothing between you and me. In this moment, for this day, we will call each other, Standing-with-Nothing-Between.

I know your Beloved-ness. Not perfection or even rightness. Beloved-ness. Embraced by the One, which having all, knowing all, chooses to love you. The oil from your hands. The texture of your hair. The sound of your voice in your language.

I recognize and need the beloved-ness for my spiritual growth. It is the beginning of seeing each other, individuals and cultures, through the eyes of God.

I am so sorry for what has been done to *you*. I am sorry for what has been done to the beloved-ness of the Standing-before-me-person-with-nothing-between.

I come to you to ask you to be my relative, to be the one I call brother, sister, grandmother, grandfather, son, or daughter. I come to say that in our community, you will never be an orphan, or alone, or your children without family.

You will sing my songs. You will tell my stories. You will share of my food. We will sing to a new dawn.

I will never put myself over you or others. Instead, I will speak of your good works, so that others will know you.

We have agreed that we are in this for good, completely together in prayer. If God says someone or something is okay, it's okay. God doesn't play favorites. Beloved Community.

Because you are my brother, my sister, I will say to others, "What about my sister? What about my brother?"

Like God, I have scratched your name upon the palm of my hand as a sign of how much I have chosen to love you.

We have agreed . . .
We have agreed that we are in this for good . . .
. . . completely together in prayer.
If God says it is okay. It's okay.
God doesn't play favorites.
There is a singing to a new dawn; a vision for beloved community.

Notes

1. These and the similarly hyphenated words in the rest of this chapter are by choice. English is not always the first or primary language of Native people. I would like for Native readers' first focus to be on relationship in each of these root words. Often, when we teach Native children, we use the hyphen to link words, which results in the "giving of a name," to a person, persons, or situations.

2. Lewis, *The Problem of Pain* (London: Centenary Press, 1940), 49–50.

3. Lewis Evely, *That Man Is You*, trans. Edmond Bonin (Westminster, MD: Newman Press, 1966).

For Further Reading

Noley, Homer. *First White Frost: Native Americans and United Methodism.* Nashville: Abingdon Press, 1991.

Fassett, Thom, White Wolf. *Giving Our Hearts Away: Native American Survival.* United Methodist Women, 2008.

CHAPTER TWO

A Tapestry in the Disanga: Building Beloved Community from a Congolese Perspective

J. Kabamba Kiboko

Personal Journey

In introducing myself, I would say the most significant aspect of my life is that I am a native of the Democratic Republic of the Congo (DRC), Central Africa. I am a Musanga, meaning that I was born into the Basanga people (Basanga is the plural form of Musanga). We live in the southern area of the Katanga province and speak the Kisanga language. The term Disanga has three different aspects: an etymological, an historical, and a geographic aspect. Etymologically, the term comes from the verbal form kusanga, which means to meet and the verbal form *kuisanga*, which means to meet together. The Disanga is then a crossroads or a place of gathering, a place of togetherness. The Basanga think of it etymologically as simply a place at the crossroads. Historically, the definition arises from the physical location itself. The Disanga is also known as the *Disanga nyama na Bantu* meaning the gathering of animals and people. Finally, geographically, a stream exists in the Disanga called the Kasanga, which runs through the center of the land and ties two rivers together. Thus, Disanga also means the territory where the stream, the Kasanga, is at its center. There are approximately 1.5 million Basanga. In its broadest meaning, then, the Basanga are all those who speak the Kisanga language.

I was born in the late 1950s, when the Congo was occupied by colonial Belgium, and was called *Congo Belge* (the Belgian Congo). I was raised in three cultures: one is my Basanga culture, another is my larger Central African culture where Kiswahili (Swahili) is now one of the primary regional languages, and the last is my imperial culture that was brought by the Belgians, who colonized the Congo in the late 1800s and brought the French language and Francophone culture to my people. I lived geographically as a child at a crossroads. I lived historically through a crossroads in the Congo as it moved to independence in 1960. I now live in a post-colonial place between Africa and the West. This has had religious implications for my life. My family clearly identified with a number of aspects of the ancient Basanga way(s) of life (avoiding using the term religion, which does not exist in my language). My parents were also devoted Roman Catholics, and these two traditions stood together and intermingled despite the protests of the church hierarchy and its representatives. Eventually, I converted to United Methodism as a teenager after an indescribable experience of the divine power that led me to confess and accept Jesus Christ as my Lord and Savior. I have, therefore, known what it is to live under European colonization and to live in a postcolonial state. I now live in the United States near Houston, Texas.

I am, however, more than a Musanga ex-pat. I am a ground-breaking clergywoman in the Southern Congo Episcopal Area of The United Methodist Church, a UM clergy spouse, a mother of two college-attending children, and a newly degreed scholar of the Old Testament. I was educated in both the DRC and the USA, and have been a UM pastor in the Southern Congo Conference and in the Texas Conference. I now serve a predominantly Anglo congregation in Katy, Texas, after having served predominantly African American congregations in the Texas Conference. I have additionally been serving as a mission interpreter and liaison for the Southern Congo Episcopal Area since 1986 and also as a translator (English-Swahili-French) for the General Conference of The UMC since 1996. I speak and read many African, European, and ancient Near Eastern languages. I move across languages and country borders. I live and work at the intersection of the northern and southern hemispheres—an unusual mission field, within which I hear multiple voices seeking to shape the discourse in the global United Methodist Church. I am all of these.

The Basanga people are storytellers, and, therefore, I am a tapestry of stories and traditions, woven from the strands of many stories—the stories of my Musanga mother, living relatives, and ancestors in the DRC, the stories of my nation, the stories of Africa as a whole, the stories of my churches and church members in both the DRC and the USA, the stories of the global UMC, the stories of the communion of saints, the stories of America, and many others. My tapestry, therefore, sits at the intersection of, or in the space between, DRC and the USA. My tapestry rests in the *disanga* of Africa and the West. My tapestry faces, however, another tapestry, one of racism, colonialism, imperialism, religionism, nationalism, tribalism, and sexism. It is a tapestry of demoralization that exists in the DRC, in Africa, and, in reality, across the globe. I seek in my life and ministry to resist this painful tapestry in favor of the positive elements of life, which stem from the love of God.

Within these many contexts, I have, indeed, experienced God's love. It is always present, both inside and outside of our connectional church, The UMC. I know it even in the DRC. These lived experiences constitute the foundation upon which the present reflection is built. I accepted the invitation to participate in this resource, in part, because of my experiences with the loving tapestry built by God and from my personal life experience and those of others. My other motivation stems from how desperately our connectional church, The UMC, needs to know beloved community. I believe that God is working to bring beloved community to our denomination and to all of humanity. I wish to be one of God's servants in this endeavor.

What I hope to do in this essay is to offer some information about my life in the Congo and the traditions of my people. Within that discussion, I will address some of the effects of the racism, colonialism, imperialism, religionism, tribalism, and sexism that I have experienced. Then I will discuss what beloved community looks like from both a biblical and my Congolese perspective and the obstacles that exist to such a community in the biblical and Congolese contexts. I will share, finally, my hope for building beloved community in spite of those obstacles.

The Basanga People and the DRC

The Basanga believe in the divine and have an understanding of their origin. The divine is Lesa. Lesa makes the ground quake. When asked "Who is God?" A Musanga (one of the Basanga people) will reply to this question by saying: *Lesa i Lesa*, "God is God." A Musanga understands Lesa through Lesa's attributes, which are: (1) *Lesa Ilunga wa bisela*, "Lesa the one who is the cause of all phenomena"; (2) *Lesa jinyinya mitumba*, "Lesa the one who shakes the mountains"; (3) *Lesa wa kupanga ne kupangulula*, "Lesa the one who constructs and deconstructs"; (4) *Lesa kapinganwa nabo*, "Lesa a Supreme Being, none other is like Lesa"; (5) *Lesa shakapanga wapangile djulu ne ntanda*, "Lesa the only one creator who created heaven and earth"; (6) *Leza na kwala kapala*, "Lesa the one who established the attic [firmament]"; (7) *Lesa kapole mwine bantu*, "Lesa the ancestor of the whole human race"; (8) *Lesa katelwa-telwa*, "Lesa the unnamable who is not to be talked about in vain"; (9) *pakumutela twatenga panshi*, "when we name Lesa, we touch the ground"; (10) *Lesa kibanza-banza Kyoto kyotelwa kulampe, kwipi wapya lubangi*, "Lesa who is a flame whose warmth one enjoys from a distance, once one approaches it, one burns"; and (11) *Lesa i wa nyake*, "Lesa is eternal." The ground on which the Basanga people walk is subjected to Lesa, who can shake it anytime. (It is significant and crucial to mention that in most African languages, there are no masculine or feminine personal pronouns. I admit that when talking about the divine, I lose something through translation.) The Basanga's way of life is understood in light of this reality. As a result, the Basanga see the necessity of learning how to walk on such a ground. The trembling of the ground is highly evocative of Yahweh, who placed (Job 38:4; Ps. 75:3) and can shake the pillars of the earth. As Samuel's mother sings in 1 Samuel 2:8):

> He raises up the poor from the dust;
>> he lifts the needy from the ash heap,
>> to make them sit with princes
>>> and inherit a seat of honor.
> For the pillars of the earth are the Lord's,
>> and on them he has set the world.

Job also reminds us:

> The pillars of heaven tremble,
>   and are astounded at his rebuke. (Job 26:11)

The Basanga's way of life is not compartmentalized; it is, rather, holistic. "Religion" encompasses every aspect of life. It is not separate from other aspects of life. There is no public / private division. Thus, I refer to the Basanga's way of life as "holism" or *Uzima* in Kiswahili. Two related fundamental principles shape the Basanga people's conceptual framework: the mbusa and the luuku. The *mbusa* is the force that runs through the belief system of the Basanga and holds them together. Basanga holism is understood through the *mbusa*, "the womb," which holds the people together and imparts wisdom to them as they learn how to walk on such a ground. The mbusa is the rule of the way of life. It is all that makes us Basanga; it is what is at the core of being human. It contains and teaches us about the supernatural and natural world (which includes four types of spirits: Lesa, the tribal ancestors [Kiluba and Beya], the ordinary spirits, and the spirits of nature), our theological and anthropological beliefs, our community (which encompasses living individuals, animals, and the spirits of the departed) and its history and social institutions, our ethics, our ritual practice, and the psychology of the human being. In brief, the *mbusa* is about our very state of existence, which, for us, includes the way we understand the cosmos, creation, and how we know what we know. The Basanga's experience of time is as a circle, with neither beginning nor end, and entangled with space. The circle of life, according to the Basanga, is a complex mixture of absent and present. This is reflected in our understanding of the departed, which I will explain in a moment. This unity, *uzima*, is assured through the ceremonies prescribed in the *mbusa*, which are performed at significant stages of life such as birth, rites of passage, marriage, conception, enthronement, and death. Women have a tremendous significance among the Basanga. The *mbusa* is entrusted primarily to a woman in each clan because the female is viewed as a good custodian, enlightened in all matters related to the way of life. This explains why the Basanga have a matrilineal and matriarchal system. The *luuku* is a combination of insights and wisdom. Both men and women are believed to have this. These two principles are to be passed on from generation to generation. They are to be remembered.

Those primarily responsible for showing the way are trained in what I term "traditional institutions"; they learn from well-trained and initiated men and women, who have been enlightened by the sages and who are able to communicate with the supernatural. The first thing such persons learn in their study is ontological in nature, as the teaching focuses on learning about their holistic identity as Basanga through the *mbusa*. Thus, those entrusted with the responsibility to tend to cultic matters are highly educated, and their responsibilities included many aspects of life, much like those cultic personnel in the ancient Israel and the greater Near East.

The female is also important in Basanga cosmological understandings: the Basanga believe that they originated from two female ancestors named Kiluba and Beya. For this reason, the Basanga are referred to as *bana ba Kiluba na Beya*, "Children of Kiluba and Beya." These two ancestors are deified and are believed to function as intermediaries and intercessors, both of whom present the people's petitions to Lesa, whom the people believe to be both present and distant at the same time. The two deified ancestors stand closer to Lesa, closer to the people, and between the living (the people) and Lesa (the Supreme Being). With such a background, it felt right to say the Catholic prayer asking Mother Mary to intercede on our behalf while I was attending Sacré-Coeur Roman Catholic Church. It felt right to recite the *Symbole des Apôtres*, in which one affirms one's faith, declares that Jesus comes to judge the living and the dead and also one affirms one's belief in the *communion of saints*. The reference to a near-deified female, the living and the dead, the communion of saints, are not alien concepts to the Basanga. Thus, they could have been talking points between the mission-church and indigenous people. Unfortunately, the indigenous way of life and its discourse was considered to be primitive and heathen.

Apart from these two ancestors of the Basanga people as a whole, ordinary ancestors of a particular clan or a family exist, who are the departed. When someone dies, we offer funerary rituals to help her or him make the transition to her or his new home with peace. These ordinary ancestors dwell in the village of ancestors, known as Kalunga or Kalunga Nyembo, "a world under the water." Our understanding of these ordinary ancestors is very much wrapped up in our understanding of time. Because time is cyclical and infinite, the departed are both absent and present, dead and living, at the same time. They died and yet continue to live in two ways, which I will discuss momentarily. This experience is an interlocking of the living and the dead. These ancestors are referred to as *bakishi* (or *mukishi* in the singular). Such ancestors are a part of the community of the Basanga and play a significant role in the social structure of our society.

The *bakishi* participate in the life of the living in two ways: through rebirth or dwelling in someone. A *mukishi* can choose to be reborn. In such case, a *mukishi* appears in a dream, mostly to barren or forsaken women, who are looked down upon because they either do not have children or their children have died. A *mukishi* would declare her or his intention to be born. The newborn baby will carry the name of the departed ancestor and will be seen as the departed ancestor, who has come back. A *mukishi*, if not reborn, can choose to make her- or himself available to be summoned through a human intermediary to provide guidance in a time of crisis. They can, for instance, be seen in dreams or apparitions. In some cases, a mukishi chooses to dwell in someone for a period. The person in whom a mukishi dwells or the person with the ability to summon a *mukishi* for guidance is enabled by such spirit to see in the beyond and tell what she or he sees. The *mukishi* speaks through the mouth of the person who summoned her or him. Thus, the individual in whom the *mukishi* dwells channels the spirit so that it may communicate with the living. In other words, the person with the ability to summon a *mukishi* has the gift of thaumaturgy. In the Basanga's worldview, *bakishi* diviners are especially important because they help the community cope with the reality that evil is in the world.

We believe that all authority has been willed by the divine; as a result, we respect those who are in authority and those who are older. This does not exclude one from humbly and respectfully speaking to those in authority. In fact, the Basanga people have a wisdom saying that shapes one's posture before one introduces any remarks to the authority figure: *Ku mutwe kwa mulopwe kujila nkoni ino diwi difika*, "To the head of a king, it is forbidden to hit, but a word can reach." One addresses this saying to the leader in all humbleness, with two hands held together as one addresses with a calm voice the wisdom saying to the authority. The saying prepares the way and always leads to a constructive conversation between the messenger and the authority.

Among the Basanga people, life itself is viewed as a ritual. As a result, their way of life is replete with rituals: rituals from the time of birth through death. The most precious and unforgettable ritual for me was the coming of age ritual, which is different for men and women. The rituals for my brothers did not last more than twenty-four hours, while mine lasted three full days, in which I was not permitted to eat, drink, or speak. Here is my account of this ritual.

One day, my mother instructed me to go to my aunt's house after school as a ruse. A few hours later, my aunt told me that we had to go back to my house because my mother was not feeling well. When we approached my house, there were a great many people. As I entered the house, a lady held me and whispered into my ears that I was the blessed one and was going to go through the rite of passage. From that moment on, I totally surrendered to the process. In fact, I was at the mercy of *bimbela*, "enlightened women," who would move me occasionally to make sure that I was in a comfortable position. My job was to stay still and listen. I listened to the songs, to the drum beats, and to the silence when no drums or music were played. I learned there to listen and to be without saying a word. On the third day at dawn, someone called my name from outside of the house. I automatically answered without anyone instructing me. I shouted, "Here I Am." Immediately, the women took me outside to hear the singing of *"Kalondo kami kadila ngele ngele kaokoka,"* "my pot made of clay sounds bing bing; it is done and ready." This means that as a pot is readied by firing, so now I, through this rite, am ready to face the challenges of the world. I then received food and water, which in my culture means that we are in agreement. In this manner, the *mbusa* and the *luuku* were entrusted to me by wise women of my clan.

In sharing a bit of my culture, one must be careful not to extrapolate this to all African cultures. One may say that some common ground exists among African indigenous ways of life, especially in their agreement regarding the existence of the world of the supernatural and the spirits, which intermingle with the world of humans and the world of matter. This does not, however, mean uniformity on the African continent. Africa is amazingly diverse in geography, ethnicity, culture, and language. In the Democratic Republic of the Congo alone, it is estimated that more than two hundred languages (not dialects) are currently in use within hundreds of ethnic groups. Each ethnic group has its own specific understandings of the supernatural and natural world. Moreover, the various life-cycle and spiritual rituals may differ among ethnic groups. Thus, we cannot reduce the whole variety of African practices on the African continent to one and, then, place it under the label, "African religion."

We hear much about the conflicts in Africa, but that is not the whole story. As a child, my family lived for some time in a city where people of many ethnic groups coexisted together away from their respective villages. Each household still practiced its individual way of life. The neighbor on our right, a native of the Kasai region, practiced blood sacrifice involving chickens, while the neighbor on our left, a native of North Katanga, practiced healing through communication with the spirits of her ancestors. Sandwiched between these two cultures, we had our own indigenous way. In spite of the fact that those of our neighborhood practiced many different African traditions, we all also attended faithfully Sacré Coeur Roman Catholic Church. Moreover, we got along. Our neighbors (including my parents) never condemned one another. Even though they were very different, with nothing in common, none of them thought themselves to be better than the other. There was neither exclusiveness nor absolutism. The real problem of our community was that the church condemned the native ways of life. The African *uzima*, the African "way(s) of life," was misinterpreted, misunderstood, and misrepresented. The self-loathing instilled by colonial, imperialist missionaries has had lasting adverse effects on the African soul.

The Colonial Past of United Methodism Is Well Alive

In the context of the mission field at the intersection of the northern and southern hemisphere, where the global United Methodist Church is shaped, the impact of racism has many complex layers. The missionary, colonial, imperial past of United Methodism is alive and well in the United States, in Europe, and on the African continent. The United Methodist Church and its predecessors in the northern hemisphere have spoken a monologue of power and authority for two centuries and imposed it on the denomination globally through its missionary offices, which have historically been in collaboration with colonial and imperial forces. It retains its colonial model. Although recently some supposed efforts have been made to redistribute power at the global level, they have been more illusory than real. Equality will come only when the western powers in the northern hemisphere share real management of the church with the countries of the South and the East.

The continent of Africa faces the historical challenges of racism, colonialism, imperialism, and the missions that were full participants in these, at two levels: internally and externally. One example is the loathing of Africans and their traditions within the church. For example, a white or African American congregation still might refuse to accept the appointment of an African pastor. Moreover, there are Africans who would welcome happily a white fellow in mission on the continent rather than to accept an African American fellow or African fellow in mission on the continent. In a presentation at Iliff School of Theology, Bishop Imathiu made an interesting observation, stating: "If I were to send a message to my country, Kenya, and tell the people that two guests—a student and a professor—are coming," pointing to an African American professor and a white student, "when they would get to my country, the people would assume that you, Professor Harding, were the student and the white student, the professor." Whiteness is still considered to be superior to blackness, and America is superior to Africa—even by Africans themselves.

Furthermore, The United Methodist Church cannot pay a native person, capable of doing the same work, what they are willing to pay a U.S.-born individual, simply because it is said that it will spark jealously from his or her own people. Thus, the church has used envy and jealousy to diminish us and continues to do so. This is a manifestation of both external and internalized racism, imperialism, and colonialism that was taught to Africans in great measure by those from Europe and North America in the African mission field. We can begin to upgrade our pay only when we allow Africans to receive pay equal to that of Americans.

We not only sell our labor too cheaply, we continue to sell our natural resources too cheaply. As I have traveled through the dusty roads of Mulungwishi, other areas of the Congo, and other countries in Africa, I have seen how mother Africa is being raped because of her natural wealth. Yesterday, it was exploitation by Europe; today, it is also by China and North America. If we are going to do business with the West, we must sell our valuable goods and land for fair prices so that we can take care of our own needs. As the situation now stands, neo-colonial powers virtually steal our resources and then offer us charity to deal with the dire poverty and uneven allocation of resources in Africa. Fair wages and prices would allow Africans to stop accepting such so-called charity, which, in fact, keeps us in bondage to the West. This, too, would reflect an increased self-esteem among Africans.

Our current self-understanding has been shaped by the missionaries of the last four centuries. We have surrendered our way of life to the missionaries, imperialists, and colonialists, who believed that we and our indigenous way of life were inferior. Christ and the Bible came to Africa, where they are much beloved. Yet the cost was the loss of many of our self-defining and unifying traditions. We were told repeatedly that we were devils or savages, who had to become like white men to become civilized and godly. Unfortunately, we could never measure up; no matter how white we were on the inside, we remained black on the outside. Ultimately, we were robbed of everything: self-worth, our way of life, our land, our resources, our ability to earn money, our very lives. Millions died in slave-like working conditions in the mines of the Congo. Rebuilding requires a shift in the self-esteem of Africans internally and vast resources to repair the damage to African nations. Africa must demand the respect and financial reparations to which it is entitled.

Mother Africa now faces her own children tearing one another down through tribalism, along with corruption, greediness, jealousy, envy, competition, and more. When only a sliver of meat or pie is available, the children will fight bitterly over it. This violent anger toward another ethnic group is nothing short of displaced rage. Instead of tackling the remnants of our missionary, colonial, imperial state—inadequate wages, poverty, economic bondage to the West, unequal distribution of recourses, corruption, a lack of education, and so forth—we engage in tribalism.

What precisely is a tribe? And what is tribalism? These terms do not exist in my language and in many other Congolese languages that I speak. In Kisanga, we speak of *bena* . . ., which is equivalent to the Hebrew term *bene*, as in *bene yisrael*, "sons of Israel." The Kisanga term *bena* means "people of." This reflects a clan that came from the same ancestors. As the family tree grows, it expands into several large entities referred to as *bena*. This is much as with Noah, who has three children: Shem, Ham, and Japheth. From the ancestor Noah, we have so many clans: Abraham the ancestor of all the Israelites comes from Shem (Genesis 11:10-26); Ham is the ancestor of the Jebusites, Amorites, Canaanites, Cushites (Ethiopians), Libyans, Egyptians, etc. (Genesis 10:6-20); and Japheth's descendants include Magog, Ashkenaz and Elishah (Genesis 10:2-5). In Israel, the twelve tribes descend from the twelve sons of Jacob. There is no real distinction between clans and tribes in the Hebrew Bible, and all are "sons of Israel." In other words, tribes are related through sonship; the many tribes are kin. Even though, in many cases, the different peoples of Africa are believed to descend from different ancestors and have different life practices, we should act like family, not like diverse ethnic groups, warring with one another. This latter behavior is common in Africa and is what I call the sin of tribalism.

We, in Africa, have a mandate to live together. We are called to be a beloved community. This mandate is even built within our language. For example, the Uruund language is spoken by people called Arund. The word *uruund* means friendship, and *arund* means friends. The Basanga, in Kisanga, are a joined, hyphenated people. Tribalism, a term foreign to these groups, has no place.

The sin of tribalism reminds me of the message preached by the late Bishop Abel Muzorewa at the Jerusalem UMC in Lubumbashi when I was serving there. In his sermon entitled "Stand Up and Walk" (based on Acts 3:6), the bishop began with a moving parable about God, who was blessing the world continent by continent, although I confess that I am unable to relate it as eloquently as he did.

God was blessing the world continent by continent, and it was all good until God was ready to bless Africa. When God got to the

African continent, it was as in the case of every other continent God had just blessed: God asked the Africans to build a human pyramid. Africans were to come together in the shape of pyramid with only one person on the very top of the human pyramid. God would then pour blessings into the hands of the one on the tip of the human pyramid and the blessings would flow throughout the pyramid reaching to everyone therein. The Africans gathered. Now, as soon as God was ready to pour the blessings, those at the base started getting curious wanting to see in whose hands God's blessings would be poured. They asked: "From which tribe is the person on the tip top?" As they moved trying to see who was on the top, the moves caused the human pyramid to collapse. They all, therefore, missed the God's blessings.[1]

The late Bishop Muzorewa challenged Africans to stand up, walk in the name of Jesus Christ of Nazareth, and begin to work as a unit that God's blessings might flow to the very foundation of the pyramid, the masses of ordinary Africans. The focus on ethnicity, with its attendant hatred and envy disrupted the flow of God's blessings. This is true in Africa.

Nevertheless, another facet of neocolonialism disrupts this flow: the base requires, in order to receive God's blessings that the top allow the blessings to flow properly. If the top dams up the blessings, keeping all that it is given by God and, thereby deprives the flow of blessings to stream toward the base, the bottom will necessarily look up and collapse. The top layer in Africa, as is clearly happening also now in America, is preventing the flow of blessings to reach us all, and this is the result of the abuse and neglect that the West has visited upon Africa in its racism and imperialism. Tribalism was not begun by colonial forces. Greed and hatred of the other are based in human sin. Yet it was greatly enhanced by colonial powers, who favored some over others and taught us hierarchy. Frankly, we are now in a vicious circle. The challenges left by colonial powers continue to enhance the internal challenge of tribalism; and tribalism continues to empower external forces to ravage Africa.

We need to stop what I call "missionism," because it has an agenda that is not disclosed to the missionized: what the missionized does is always irrelevant because he or she is viewed as someone who does not know, who must be controlled, and to whom given power must be limited. A case in point is the conclusion of the study committee on the worldwide nature of The UMC, who traveled around the globe recently to hold "listening sessions" and study how to make a more global and equitable church: "Consistency in election is critical: the diversity of term election / elections for life, re-election brings chaos to continent of Africa."[2] In the Congo, a bishop is elected for one four-year term and can run again along with other candidates. If he or she is re-elected, then, the term *"Evêque à vie"* is applied: the bishop will serve until retirement. Bishops in the USA, on the other hand, are elected immediately as bishops for life [although the term is not used. They are bishops until they retire]. We are not heard at all and are constantly told what is good for us in a context of missionism—a characteristic of institutionalized racism. Power is not equally shared. This dynamic continues in both secular and religious realms.

The Nature of Beloved Community from Biblical and Congolese Perspectives

The Old Testament offers us many clues about the nature of beloved community. The Genesis creation account of 1:1–2:4, describes a community wherein God is its center, his Word brings forth life; humans, animals, and vegetation are all purposeful. Man and woman are equal partners, co-creators with God within this community and stewards of the creation. And it was very good (1:31). Beloved community can be theologically and biblically described as a community of people who live in relationship with the LORD God and with one another (Genesis 2:15-25). Additionally, Adam and Eve lived in beloved community within the Garden of Eden (Genesis 3). Thus, beloved community is a community called into being by God and centered upon God.

Other passages teach us about the nature of beloved community. It is a place of justice (Exodus 18:19-26; Deuteronomy 1:16; 16:18); charity (Deuteronomy 15:7); moderation (Deuteronomy 15:12); and where the people are educated in God's ways (Leviticus 10:11). Psalm 133 teaches us that living in unity within beloved community is very good, as in Genesis 1:31:

How very good and pleasant it is
 when kindred live together in unity!
It is like the precious oil on the head,
 running down upon the beard,
on the beard of Aaron,
 running down over the collar of his robes.
It is like the dew of Hermon,
 which falls on the mountains of Zion.
For there the LORD ordained his blessing,
 life forevermore (Psalm 133).

Another example of people living in beloved community is found in the Acts of the Apostles. When the people heard God's word boldly preached, they responded: "What should we do?" (Acts 2:37). They were told to repent, to be baptized in the name of Jesus Christ for the forgiveness of sins. They received the Holy Spirit (v. 38) and shared everything together (v. 44). They went out of their comfort zones to reach out to others. Three thousand persons joined the group (v. 41). Such beloved community can, therefore, be described as a community of people who are in relationship with Christ and with one another. They have experienced the transforming power of God, which draws them to God and to one another.

In light of these biblical passages and my experience as a musanga, beloved community is created by God, centers on God, and allows God's transformative loving power to enter us, heal us, and teach us to love one another. It is a meeting place, a *disanga*. I mean by this a place where the earth and all its species are cherished. It is eco-friendly and treats the whole earth like the Garden of Eden. It crosses geographic, cultural, social, religious, gender, and chronological boundaries. It includes those who have gone before us (the communion of saints) and those who will follow us (our children and their descendants). It is a place where the traditions of the past have meaning and voice, yet is future-driven that we might leave the earth as the Garden for our children and their children. It is a place where different people can come to communicate on an equal footing. It is a community built on multilingual communication. It is a place of authentic, honest, and loving communication. It is a place where we speak with one another, not at one another. It is a place of learning the other's cultural values. It is a place where we hold one another in mutual respect, whether friend or stranger. It transcends, through God's love, the sins of racism, sexism, religionism, colonialism, imperialism, ethnic hatred, and tribalism. It is a place of peace not war. In sum, it, too, is a lovingly and carefully woven tapestry of the diversity of humanity and nature. A beloved community is a community that does not give charity but teaches survival skills to those who have not been permitted to function adequately due to long histories of racism and the like. Beloved community practices good steward- ship of funds in this way.

The Obstacles to Beloved Community in the Bible and the DRC

Building beloved community is hard. Even in the Bible, we see more instances of broken community than beloved community. For example, Adam and Eve were first separated from God when they hid, being naked and filled with fear (Genesis 3:10). Adam and Eve were ultimately banished from the Garden of Eden because they disobeyed God and took leadership in a greedy, prideful manner (Genesis 3:22-24). They disrespected their role as co-creators with God, seeking to be sole creators (Genesis 11:4-6). Humankind broke the community through lust for control of what only the LORD God maker could control what the LORD God has made. Humankind wants to control without following the guidance of the One who created that which humankind wants to control. We see that control issues, miscommunication, and mispresentation break community. Moreover, when God inquires about Adam and Eve's disobedience, they demonstrate their brokenness by blaming others: Adam blames Eve and Eve blames the serpent (Genesis 3:12-13).

Later in the Bible, we see more division. Family members set upon one another, as in the case of Joseph and his brothers (Genesis 37). Kin sets upon kin, as the many tribes of Israel warred with the tribe of Benjamin (Judges 20; cf. Genesis 49:27). Solomon killed half-brothers to solidify his hold on the throne (1 Kings 2:25, 44–46). Extended civil war broke out after Solomon died, and Israel eventually seceded from Judah as a nation (1 Kings 12). These are just a few of the many exemplars of broken community from the Old Testament. Paul testifies in his many letters to the difficulty the early churches had in maintaining beloved community (e.g., 1 Corinthians 1:10-13; Galatians 1:6-7). And even Jesus became discouraged from time to time with his beloved, but often confused, bewildered, and faithless disciples (Matthew 17:14-21).

Another biblical example of broken community is found in the curse of Canaan narrative (Genesis 9:20-27). In this narrative, Noah is drunk and naked in his tent (v. 21). His son Ham sees Noah's nakedness. When Noah learns that his son, Ham, saw his nakedness, Noah curses Ham's son, Canaan, because Ham saw his nakedness. Canaan is to be a servant of servants to his brothers (v. 25). Canaan is cursed by his grandfather for the action of his father. Among Ham's children are Cush, Egypt, Put, and Canaan.

This example of broken community has deeply and negatively affected Africa and the African diaspora. A review of literature on the history of interpretation of the curse of Canaan account indicates that from 1500 to 1860 Europeans and Euro-Americans used this narrative to validate enslavement of Africans. Although its usage was mostly during the colonial period, it was very much en vogue in the nineteenth-century discourse on slavery. It was used as a biblical proof to justify the inferiority of Africans. This raises many exegetical, theological, and cultural questions. Does the text, Genesis 9:18-27, in fact, lend itself to such claims? Does this text lend itself to be a proof-text for white supremacy? Does it favor colonization? Does it favor tribalism? How does Noah, God's man, help us see the greatness of his God? Does Noah's action help us understand a relational and loving God? What place does this text have in our current culture? Let us examine these questions very briefly.

Genesis 9:18-27 clearly highlights that Noah has cursed his grandson Canaan, youngest son of Ham. Canaan has three big brothers: Cush, Egypt, and Put. It is evident that the Hebrew "Cush" is translated as Ethiopia (twenty-five times) and "Kushi" as Ethiopians (four times). In Jeremiah 13:23, we read: "Can Ethiopians change their skin or leopards their spots?" In most occurrences of this Hebrew word, it clearly is referring to Ethiopians. The text when read in the context of the Old Testament, the reader is informed that Canaan's brother Cush was an Ethiopian. If Cush was Ethiopian, then his brothers Egypt, Put, and Canaan were of the same skin color and all from Africa. Put is usually understood to be modern-day Libya. This means that their father Ham—and their uncles Shem and Japheth—were of the same skin color, and thus the grandfather Noah was of the same skin. Does this text lend itself to be a proof-text for white supremacy? It does not. Does it favor colonization? It does not since colonization, as we have experienced it, involves whites colonizing other races. Instead of justifying white supremacy, this text could more readily easily be used to describe and explain the tribalism that Africans continue to experience. The text is clear that Noah's descendants will live at odds with one another.

This text demonstrates what is happening in the context of Africa where tribalism prevails. There is a pressing need in the DRC to build beloved community, this disanga, where mutual respect and love embrace. Unfortunately, many challenges to this exist. Those obstacles form a different, competing tapestry to that of beloved community: a painful tapestry of bias, discrimination, and persecution, forming the "isms" of racism, colonialism, imperialism, tribalism, sexism, and more. This sad tapestry has complexities and nuances that make it difficult to isolate its various strands. The impact of this tapestry is easy to see, however, as the DRC has been engaged in armed conflict for most of the twentieth and twenty-first centuries. The atrocities are staggering and, within the postcolonial situation, are based especially in both sexism and tribalism, which has been exaggerated by racism, colonialism, and imperialism. The incidence of conflict rape is the largest ever documented in history. In November 2011, we had a national election in the Congo and once again violence erupted. A pregnant woman was beaten to the point where she miscarried and was still being beaten because she belongs to a different region. It is difficult to express such atrocities. My heart weeps for all the victims. My voice cries out "Peace, peace" (Isaiah 57:19). I long for the day when my family and neighbors all love and respect one another despite our difference.

The world at large also has a pressing need for beloved community. We are destroying the climate and ecosystems of our planet and many species of life. The rainforests are being plowed under to reach top soil for agriculture. Alas, without the rain forest the top soil quickly deteriorates and blows away. Droughts and floods of global warming are killing us and will eventually lead to mass migrations. There is also no time in recorded history when the entire planet has known peace: somewhere in the world at least two groups have been at war. Moreover, war is a game wherein both parties must lose. The victor is, unfortunately, no more than the group who suffered the least amount of death and destruction. Satan wins a lot of battles, but he always wins a garbage heap. The only way to win the war is to give up the war because only God's love builds up (e.g., Isaiah 61:4; 1 Thessalonians 5:11). If we focus on God, we can build instead of inflicting wholesale destruction on entire cultures and countries.

My Hope for Beloved Community

I see glimmers of hope and am not discouraged. I remember keenly the lessons that I learned when walking with my mother during my childhood. One is particularly important for this reflection. We would travel from one village to another through a narrow path—with me in front and my mother right behind me. The grass was very tall on both sides of the path, and I felt as though the bush would just gobble me up—and maybe already had! We would hear animal noises during the entire journey, and I was constantly reminded that we were journeying through the animals' world. During the first of these trips, I walked just a few steps forward, stopped suddenly, and then ran backward into my mother because I was just too overwhelmed to go on. I remember that, later, we saw a snake cross the path. Mother and I stopped until the snake crossed. We then continued on our way. Mother told me, "Keep your mind on the destination: the village where we are going. If you keep your mind on the noises all around us in this bush, you will never make it to the destination." The journey of life is not an easy one either. We encounter obstacles that overwhelm us, things that frighten us, and real dangers along the way. Many of the frightening and dangerous things along the way to beloved community are a result of racism, colonialism, imperialism, tribalism, sexism, missionism, and other isms. In building beloved community, we must keep our eye on the village, the disanga, the community itself, and not the obstacles and fears along the way. God's love calls us to this place of peace.

Another hopeful sign exists within The UMC, where God has provided such a place of encounter, a *disanga*, where citizens of nations who are hostile to one another (e.g., Rwanda, Burundi, and the DRC) may come together. I see this in Africa University, with its mandate to be a *disanga* where all nationalities are called to think beyond tribe and nation, but to join together for the betterment of self and Africa at large. If we can do it there, we can do it on a still larger scale.

Sometimes, instead of Jesus' golden rule, we live by this golden rule: "He who has the gold makes the rules." In Africa, we follow blindly the authority of the rich whether they are in our homeland or in the West. We wait for charity to trickle down to the needy instead of building up Africa so that all may earn a fair wage and have self-respect. It appears that, until the church in Africa generates its own funds, the church in the USA will treat African leaders as charity cases and, therefore, second-class leaders. I do not want America or The UMC to hand me a fish once in a great while, when I can learn to fish, and there are fish aplenty to be caught due to God's blessing grace. We have to give up this unhelpful golden rule and embrace Jesus' message to love the neighbor, the stranger, and even the enemy. If we return to Bishop Muzorewa's parable of the pyramid of blessings, those at the top must believe that they are not a deserving few entitled alone to God's blessings; they are stewards of God's blessings for all the people. In that stewardship, they are to let the blessings flow to all.

We Africans must also remember who and whose we are. My mother, who never went to school, always reminded me that I have to remember who I am and value our *mbusa* and *luuku*: "You can never understand the Bible if you do not know your own culture, if you do not know who you are and thus miss your purpose." The Bible, mother insisted, was written in a certain culture: "*Leza kenshi walembele bibule*," "God did not write the Bible." Most of our ways of life were eroded. We gradually became a "translated people."[3]

We cannot go back and undo the violations of the past. we can go forward in a postcolonial rather than neocolonial state of being. We can reclaim ourselves, our self-esteem, our African heritage, our power to make things happen, our creativity to solve problems, our ability to be co-creators with God. God's love empowers all of this. How can we be a church and survive when so many of us are getting lost in and through translation? We do not have to remain wholly translated beings, but we can speak in multiple voices. The Bible can speak to us in our own culture. In fact, the Bible shares much with African cultures and speaks to us best when we know ourselves. Where Jesus lives, there is mutual respect.

Auto-sustainability—for which Bishop Katembo Kainda has been calling throughout his episcopal area (South Congo)—is a must if we are going to be a beloved community. Missionism and charity have to be replaced by instruction in living functionally in the modern postcolonial world. Africa must become better stewards of its land in order to feed its people. Africa has a crying need for medical supplies, especially to fight malaria and AIDS. Africa needs educational resources and printed materials in our native languages. We can recognize that every people and their languages are a sign and a gift, which we can use to build beloved community. The colonial languages—Dutch, English, French, German, Italian, Portuguese—are fine, but there is a need to own our identity as embodied in our languages. One's language shapes one's conceptual framework. Africa needs better access to electricity and technology of all types. Africa must become a real player in the global economy. All of this is necessary for auto-sustainability. For this to happen, the West must give up condescension, charity, and missionism. Rather, helping Africa to help itself is the only viable agenda now. In entering beloved community with Africa, we can do this. The church belongs to Jesus Christ. He is the Master. Repentance is the key. We need to go back to the basics of Jesus' teachings. Change needed in the church should be coming from the people in the pews.

Notes

1. This is me, Kabamba, retelling Bishop Muzorewe's parable used in his sermon at Jerusalem UMC to illustrate the situation in Zaire (now Congo). I was pastor of that church at that time.

2. It will be helpful to cite the title of the study, the publisher, and the year. If it is available online, a web address would also be welcome information.

3. To be a postcolonial subject is to be a translated being. Salman Rushdie captures this experience of living postcolonially in a diaspora perfectly: "and he exists in the West in a translation that is really a complete reworking of his verses, in many cases very different from the spirit

(to say nothing of the content) of the original. I, too, am a translated man. I have been borne across. It is generally believed that something is always lost in translation; I cling to the notion . . . that something can also be gained." Salman Rushdie, *Shame* (New York: Alfred A. Knopf, 1983), 29.

For Further Reading

Innis, John G. *By the Goodness of God: An Autobiography.* Nashville: Abingdon Press, 2003. [Innis is the United Methodist Bishop of Liberia.]
Abrahams, Ivan. "To Serve the Present Age, Our Calling to Fulfill," in *Our Calling to Fulfill.* Nashville: Kingswood Books, 2009. [Abrahams is the Bishop of the Methodist Church of South Africa.]

CHAPTER THREE

Building Beloved Community: The Church in the Midst of Racism—A U.S. Latino/Hispanic Perspective

David Maldonado Jr.

Most of us are products of lives lived within communities and societies in which race has played a critical role in shaping major social institutions, whether it be government, business, education, or the church. Likewise, race has been a critical element shaping social attitudes and perceptions, as well as defining social relations and interactions among the various peoples. In essence, race has been a dominant element in the social fabric of many nations and especially in North America and its institutional history. In America, race has defined and shaped the lives of all Americans. For the dominant white population, racial structures and practices have usually meant privilege. For non-white populations such as Hispanics and Latinos, race has resulted in differential treatment, lower socioeconomic status, and other forms of marginalization.

In the United States, the Latino/Hispanic population has historically been defined as a "minority" population due to its ethnicity as well as to its racial compositions. As a population, Latinos/Hispanics historically have been treated as a racial group, though the actual racial composition of the population is not always distinctly different from the dominant population. Yet, as a broadly mestizo (European/indigenous) and mulatto (European/African) population, Latinos/Hispanics have been viewed through racial lenses, and thus subject to racial prejudice and racism.

However, Latinos represent a diversity of racial composition, ethnicities, and national cultures. For example, among some Caribbean populations there is a significant African element that is reflected not only in racial composition, but also in music, foods, health practices, and religious expressions. In Central America and reflected in immigrants from that area, the population reflects a stronger presence of indigenous roots that are also manifested in racial composition, language, foods, music, and other cultural expressions. In fact, there is a significant indigenous population in Central America, southern Mexico, and other parts of Latin America that has maintained its original racial composition and cultural ways untouched by European influences. Some of these indigenous (Mayans, for example) populations are part of the immigration flow into the United States and do not speak Spanish or English but rather speak indigenous languages. Yet, in other parts of Latin America there is a much stronger reflection of European cultural and racial sources such as Italians in Uruguay, Argentina, and Chile in the lower continent.

Yet all are Latino, share the Spanish language, have experienced Catholicism in their historical/contextual backgrounds, and share broad levels of identity as Latinos. However, in Latin America, national identity and pride are very important. Each nation has developed unique characteristics in language, foods, music, and other expressions of culture. Nationality is a strong source of self-identity and pride. Yet when they enter the United States, most are immediately categorized as "Hispanic" and are perceived and treated the same. This has led to many instances of confusion, misunderstanding, and resentment. Categorization into one ethnic (Hispanic) slot, disregards unique national cultures, racial compositions, and identities. It can also lead to problematic issues in carrying out ministry among such a diverse population due to variations of identity, language use, and other cultural expressions.

Another common misperception of Hispanics is that they are all immigrants, even though the great majority of the U. S. Hispanic population is native born, many for several generations and others for hundreds of years. Yet they are treated as outsiders and as not really belonging here. They are not treated as Americans and are expected to prove their citizenship. Not only are many individuals perceived and treated as immigrants; total Hispanic populations are defined as such. Because of language, names, race, and cultural characteristics, Latinos are assumed to be immigrants, and if they are immigrants they are also assumed to be "illegal." Recent anti-immigrant attitudes and actions such as immigration laws in Arizona and Mississippi have defined Latino immigrants as criminals and unlawful. They have been denied common public and human rights and treatment, and are subject to deportation. Thus, Latino immigrants live in fear and hiding. They are the subjects of public disdain.

Although the Latino/Hispanic population predates white settlements within the boundaries of the present United States, it is traditionally perceived as a foreign and immigrant population. The first Spanish settlements in New Mexico were established before the English pilgrims arrived on the eastern shores. However, through the Anglo American western expansion and military force, fueled by the racial ideology of manifest destiny, the Hispanic populations of New Mexico, Texas, Colorado, Arizona, and California, came under the control of American political and military forces and eventually became part of the United States. In actuality, the US-Mexican border crossed over a well-established Hispanic population. Upon conquest, the Hispanic population became defined as a foreign population with undesirable racial, religious, and cultural elements. The established Mexican population became perceived and treated as an inferior racial group with an inferior culture and especially with a false religion—Catholicism. The conquered population became a minority population that lost status, lands, and other privileges and protections of citizenship. The story of this population has been a historic struggle to survive and to regain its dignity, citizens' rights, and cultural respect, while overcoming deeply held racial and social attitudes by the dominant population.

Puerto Rico became a part of the American domain also through military means. As a result of the Spanish American war, Puerto Rico became an American territory and continues to be so. As a result, its population is American in citizenship with full rights including free movement between Puerto Rico and the mainland. However, when entering and residing in the mainland, they are treated as different, and many times their citizenship is misunderstood and questioned. Their racial, linguistic, and cultural expressions are used to define them as a minority group.

Other Latino populations have become part of the United States populace through legal immigration and as refugees. Legal immigrants from Latin America have historically been part of the American immigrant experience since the very beginning of the country. Geographic proximity and the presence of Latinos in the United States have facilitated Latino immigration. For decades the boundary between Mexico and the United States was not debated and controlled. Individuals and families freely moved back and forth between the two nations. Thus, the southern boundary became an area of high Hispanic presence from Texas to California.

Other Latino populations have come to the United Sates as political refugees. Of special significance is the Cuban American population. Due to the Cuban revolution, the United States government facilitated and welcomed a large Cuban refugee population with much political support and assistance. This population was originally concentrated in south Florida, especially the first generation. With subsequent generations, this population has grown in other geographic areas of the US. Although the first wave of refugees reflected a high European racial composition, later immigrants reflected more African influence.

Thus, the present Hispanic population is a highly diverse population with numerous nations of origin represented, each with strong identities and special characteristics such as racial composition, linguistic variations, music, foods, and other cultural expressions. Racial composition varies from highly African to indigenous and many combinations in between, including many who are highly European in composition. The Spanish that is spoken is equally varied with numerous special usages and linguistic expressions. Foods reflect the varied agricultural products of coastal areas, deserts, tropics, and mountainous regions as well as huge climate differences. The same can be said about the variation of music, customs, and even religious expressions. Yet a broad sense Latino is common, especially in the United States, where the social context perceives all Latinos as being the same and as a different population from the dominant white American population. Being thrust into a common Hispanic category while, at times, resented, also serves to unite a broad set of peoples who experience many social challenges simply because they are Hispanic/Latino.

As a member of this population I am so defined, perceived, and treated by the dominant population. Some of that treatment has become more subtle yet real, as I moved into professional and even religious settings. As a child, and as many of my family and community continue to experience, I too have experienced the consequences of racism toward Latinos and Hispanics in the United States. I am the product of a segregated neighborhood, separate schools, segregated public places, and tense group relations. I am the product of a Hispanic Methodist congregation of the era before the Civil Rights Movement. Thus, the invitation to participate in this project speaks deeply to who I am and what I have known.

I am a Latino of Mexican American heritage. I am a Tejano. I am also a product of The United Methodist Church. As a fourth generation Methodist, I have known, served, and loved the church as much as any one of my brothers and sisters in the faith. I first knew the Methodist church as a segregated institution. In my hometown there were three Methodist congregations: Wesley Harper Chapel where our African American brothers and sisters gathered for worship and fellowship. There was also First United Methodist Church that was primarily all white and was a place for them to also gather for worship and fellowship. And then there was La Trinidad Iglesia Metodista where my family, friends, and fellow believers gathered for worship and to seek fellowship.

Growing up in La Trinidad Iglesia Metodista was a special experience for me and for most of my fellow Hispanic Methodists. ("Growing Up Hispanic and Protestant," New Mexico Press). To be Methodist in the Hispanic cultural environment meant to be a Protestant in a strong Catholic ethnic and cultural context. That was not easy. We were a religious minority in the Hispanic ethnic context. Many Hispanic Protestants were shunned by family and community because of their Protestantism. To be Methodist and Hispanic involved paying a social price. You were distinguished as a *protestante* and many times ridiculed as an *aleluya*. Our church building was said to be the place of the devil and to be avoided by all good Hispanic Catholics. Thus, to be Methodist was a special identity and social experience among Hispanics.

To be Methodist and Hispanic also meant to be Hispanic in a denomination that was dominated by the white population. Within The United Methodist Church, we were an ethnic/racial minority.

We were different from most other Methodists. As we traveled to other towns and cities, the only Methodist churches that we saw were white. We worshiped in a separate church and in our own language. Not only were we separated during the pre–Civil Rights Era, but also after the 1968 General Conference, when efforts were more intentionally made to incorporate minorities into the life of the church, Hispanics continued to be marginalized within the structures of the church. To be Hispanic and Methodist meant to be a minority and marginal population within the church that meant so much to us and for which we had paid such a deep social price.

Yet, I remember my Hispanic Methodist church, its members, its life, and activities as a special place and community. When society told us that we did not belong and that it was not ours, the church told us that it was our church and that we belonged. It gave us a sense of belonging and ownership. When we were marginal in our communities, the church provided a place where we were the leadership. The minority church provided models of leadership. It was our church, and it was the center of our religious and social life. When society told us that we were inferior and undesirable, the church told us that God loved us and that we were created in God's image. Our small Hispanic church helped us to survive and overcome the pain and ravages of racism and segregation. It was an immense instrument for our survival.

I have known and experienced the church from segregation days to today when we, as United Methodists seek repentance but also guidance as we long to be a beloved community of believers known as The United Methodist Church. This will require not only grace and forgiveness but also repentance from the whole church.

Racial Attitudes and Racism in Methodist History

The story of the Methodist Church and the Hispanic/Latino population reflects many of the same social and racial dynamics and realities found in the broader society and its historical context. Methodism came to the western and southwestern regions, where the Latino population was then settled, during the western expansion of Anglo Americans. Notions of Manifest Destiny, which proposed that taking control of all territory from the Eastern seaboard to the Pacific Ocean was divinely ordained, fueled this expansion.

In addition, there was the arrogant sense that the Anglo American people, their culture, and their protestant religion were far superior to the Mexican people and culture, and to Roman Catholicism. The Mexican people were perceived as inferior, especially because they had intermarried with the Indian "savages."

Methodism arrived in the western and southwestern areas, with the intention of ministering not to the Spanish-speaking Mexicans but to the Anglo settlers and American soldiers. The memoirs of Rev. Thomas Harwood clearly express these early intentions. However, the presence of Spanish-speaking Mexicans could not be ignored, nor could they be kept from learning about Protestantism. In fact, initial contacts between Methodism and Mexicans came from the initiative of Mexicans who were curious of the protestant faith. They had heard the music and read the Bible in Spanish and were seeking to learn more. Dissatisfaction with the Catholic Church, its lack of adequate ministry among the Mexicans in the northern frontiers, and the distance from Catholic leadership, led many Mexicans to consider Protestantism. Once Protestants began to distribute Spanish Bibles, open schools, and initiate churches, Catholic leadership aggressively fought Protestant efforts. In many cases, such efforts, especially in trying to keep the Bible out of the hands of Mexicans and to prohibit Mexican children from attending Protestant schools backfired and many Mexicans turned to the Protestant churches.

Methodist ministry among the Spanish-speaking population quickly emerged as a separate ministry from the English-language ministries in Texas, New Mexico, Arizona, and California. Separate structures were established. Whether such was the case because of language, culture, or economics can be debated. But what can be noted is that separation quickly became the norm, and it did not necessarily result in equality or mutuality. On the contrary, ministries among the Latino/Hispanic populations, as missionary conferences as well as in annual conferences, have always struggled with limited human and financial resources. But what made separation more painful and sad was a pervasive lack of cooperation, fellowship, or mutuality between the geographic annual conferences (historically white annual conferences) and the Spanish language annual conferences such as the Rio Grande Annual Conference. This was especially true during the pre–Civil Rights

Era prior to the 1960s. For many years there was a sense of alienation with very little contact and relationship. A sad experience was to observe Latino pastors, many of whom were former seminary colleagues, serve in different annual conferences and receive painfully different support because Latinos were serving Hispanic congregations within the Hispanic structures. To commit to Hispanic ministry within the Spanish language annual conferences, meant lifelong poverty for the pastor and family.

In addition to the Rio Grande Conference, it is also important to note that many Hispanics have historically immigrated to other parts of the nation, initially settling in areas such as Florida, the New York–Boston area, and Chicago for example. Today, Hispanic presence is known throughout the nation, especially as the result of recent immigration. However, of special significance is that among both historic and recent immigration, Latino immigrants arrived already with Protestant or even Methodist backgrounds. In addition, many have arrived with a disposition toward and openness to Protestantism. United Methodist ministry to Latino immigrants has seen success in new places such as Wisconsin, Georgia, Tennessee, Iowa, and so on. United Methodist Hispanic congregations are emerging throughout the country in places not normally or historically considered Hispanic. As a result, there are United Methodist Hispanic congregations throughout the nation. Annual conferences in these areas, with technical assistance and support from the National Plan for Hispanic Ministries, have worked hard and effectively through conference coordinators to make impressive the presence of Hispanic ministries and congregations in these new areas.

United Methodism's Continuing Struggles

United Methodists played an active and vocal role during the Civil Rights movement that sought to overcome generations of segregation. Many white pastors and laity joined ethnic and racial persons to march and advocate for the elimination of racist segregation and lack of civil rights. The United Methodist Church invested in many initiatives to combat racism in our public places, policies, and institutional structures. However, many of these initiatives were controversial, such as the Fund for Reconciliation approved by the General Conference of 1968. This fund is an example of a United Methodist initiative to address historic issues of racism by providing support to minority community organizations and activities to overcome racism and historic marginalization. This UM fund was deeply resented by many white churches and emerged as a controversial point of contention. Through this fund and other mission initiatives, The United Methodist Church invested in making a difference and in empowering minority populations. Through the work of the Commission on Religion and Race, especially, and in spite of internal criticism, The United Methodist Church has stayed firm in the public struggle to fight racism in law, business, public schools, and other institutions, including its own life, structures, and ministry.

The United Methodist Church as we know it today, however, has not fully entered the promised land of the beloved community where God's love and grace guide and shape our lives as a church and as congregations. As a church we continue to struggle with the signs of racism, such as prejudice, lack of acceptance, denial of affirmation, and differential treatment. We still struggle with the same demons with which the ancients struggled. This is especially true at the local level. Many of our congregations live in fear of racially changing communities and resent having strange people coming to "our" churches. There is suspicion and fear of immigrants and persons of other cultures and languages. Other languages and cultural expressions are not fully welcomed. There is fear that immigrants will soil or overrun our churches, and that they will take over our churches. Many of our United Methodist brethren unfortunately view undocumented Latino immigrants through lenses that define them as criminals. Thus, Hispanic ministries have a difficult time receiving the full and enthusiastic support of the churches. Hispanic ministries are many times treated like "projects" and relegated to the basement or other settings that demean.

However, it is also important to recognize that many white pastors and congregations have taken courageous steps in welcoming and supporting Hispanic ministries within their communities and buildings, including ministries to the undocumented. This is especially true in states and regions where there are pronounced anti-immigrant sentiments and even laws, such as in Arizona, Alabama, and Mississippi. Many white pastors and congregations are taking positions and action that are indeed at odds with other congregations and even with state laws.

Currently, the Rio Grande Annual conference is the only United Methodist annual conference committed totally to the Latino/Hispanic population. However, historic economic realities of this population, limited resources, and poor finances have challenged Hispanic congregations and the viability of ministry as a conference. Sadly, the Rio Grande Conference has reached a difficult decision. In spite of its historic mission and commitment to Hispanic ministries, it voted in 2012 to merge with the Southwest Texas Conference. It remains to be seen just how the merger will impact Hispanic ministries and the historic leadership of the Rio Grande Conference within United Methodism and its ministry among the Hispanic population. Many challenges remain for The United Methodist Church in the post–Rio Grande Conference era without the special presence and witness of the Rio Grande Conference to the rest of the church of the historic struggle to minister with the Hispanic population in the context of continuing racial and ethnic challenges.

The Rio Grande Conference is rooted in the early work of the Methodist church in Texas and in New Mexico, as well as in northern Mexico in the 1800s. In fact, for a while the Hispanic work along the Mexican border was quite integrated with the Mexican church. In 1939 the Rio Grande Conference came into being. Although this conference was born in the days of segregation and separation, it fought for the right to exist and to provide some degree of self-determination. Many members of this conference fear that merger with other conferences will mean even more marginalization within the life and structures of the church. It will mean the death of a historic effort. We wait to see how this scenario will develop.

There are some signs of hope. The National Plan for Hispanic Ministries has provided critical leadership, training material, and advocacy on behalf of Latinos throughout the church and nation. Annual conferences throughout the nation have been encouraged and challenged to initiate Hispanic ministries, and some conferences have responded. These ministries are in small town and rural areas as well as in urban situations. Of special interest is a ministry response to the dramatic growth of the Hispanic population throughout the nation due to immigration from Mexico as well as other parts of Latin America. Communities and United Methodists across the land want to respond. However, there is much resistance and concern, and threat of under support. Continuing fear and criminalization of Latino immigrants, fueled by many public voices, have led to much reluctance to fully embrace the immigrant, especially the undocumented.

Contextual Forces and Realities: Challenges beyond the Church

In some societies, race and ethnicity play public and even official roles, while in other societies, they are more unspoken and subtle. In the case of the United States in the post–Civil Rights Era—when segregation, discrimination, and other forms of racial behaviors are unlawful—race has become a subtler and quieter dynamic. Racism and especially policies based on race and ethnicity are not normally accepted openly and publicly. However, this does not mean that race is no longer a powerful force. It means only that people and institutions find other means of maintaining separation, power, and privilege. Unfortunately, such is the case with religious institutions as well. The United Methodist Church is not immune to such quiet racism. Race and ethnicity is the "elephant in the room" no one seems to want to recognize, much less address. However, it is an elephant that seems to be fed not only by internal fears and reluctance but also by the larger context in which the church lives and operates. It is a sad commentary that social and political issues such as anti-immigration movements in Arizona and other states, tend to shape much of our fears, perceptions, and actions. It would seem that the church would want to lead and transform the world rather than be transformed by racist fears and ideologies in our society.

The United States of America continues to be a society solidly grounded in its racial history and formation. Racist ideologies have not only survived, they have gained strength. It seems that the election of an African American president has fueled new fears and unmasked many racial attitudes that were thought to be dormant. The immigration debate carried out in the media, the streets, and in legislative arenas is a good example of how racial attitudes have exploded once again. Our Methodist episcopal leadership has spoken eloquently against the resurgence of racism. However, our local churches are not isolated from such fear. Overt and subtle racial rhetoric penetrate our walls. As a church, we continue to officially fight against powerful voices of fear and hate in our communities and broader environment as well as within church walls. However, racism is a tremendous social force that penetrates our resistance and sneaks up on us when we least expect it.

The Human and Divine Narrative in the Bible: Struggles with Living in Community

The biblical narrative is the story of the human struggle to live in beloved community. The stories of the ancients are narratives of a human community wrestling with the realities of human sin, imperfection, and wrongdoing whether personal or social. In the Old Testament, stories of brother against brother, people against people, and nation against nation, form the early human narrative of sin, brokenness, and division. From the very beginning, the human family was thrown into division and alienation, including violence and anger within the human family. The creation that was brought into being in God's image became a source of sorrow for God. Sin broke into the human reality and condition. Human action broke God's vision and hope for a creation that was good and just. Instead of a human community centered on God's love and grace, humanity built its own world on foundations of division, greed, power, and conquest. Left to our desires, we build a world of ethnocentric societies that function out of self-interest and desire for power and control over others. Fear and prejudice against those different from oneself became the norm and guiding force. The sin of human fear, disdain and hatred toward others based on race and ethnicity—whether at the individual or group levels—have created our sinful human condition today. Racism is a form of human sin.

Yet, in the midst, or maybe because of such painful and ugly realities, "the beloved community" or "the community of love," has emerged as a divine call to humanity and a deeply held dream and vision among people of faith. To some extent, the Ten

Commandments were indicative of how humans might live with one another in community. Not meant to be exhaustive, they did provide a glimpse of a moral and ethical community of mutual respect, justice, and mutuality. The call was to live under God's vision for humanity.

The core assumption of the Ten Commandments is that humanity is a social creation. As God's creation, we are meant to live in community and learn to live together. Yet, the necessity for the Ten Commandments reminds us that the human community is indeed imperfect and has huge challenges to its communal life. The commandments were given to show us how we might live before God and with one another. They call for an orderly and ethical society in which justice, love, and respect are at the core of human community.

A powerful biblical example of one people subjugating another people is the story of the slavery of the Jews in Egypt. Slavery is an oppressive human action that forcibly confines the lives and possibilities of a people according to the dictates of another. Mass executions, such as Hitler's attempt to eliminate the Jews, are probably the only more oppressive human action that can and has been taken by the human family against itself. Unfortunately, mass executions and ethnic cleansing have continued today in Africa and places such as Bosnia. In the United States lynching of blacks is part of our history; today, hate crimes that involve race have become common. The racial treatment of Latinos in the United States generally did not reach such inhumane levels, although many stories of abuse in the hands of the historic Texas Rangers have survived. However, the biblical story of God's action to free the enslaved people from their oppression is a reminder that God's call for freedom and justice will not cease until the divine mandate is heard and carried out. Today, God calls us to free all people from oppressions, especially the oppression of racism and hatred.

Jesus came into a society deeply divided along ethnic and religious lines. He was acutely aware of it. It was into such a society that God sent his son to reveal our divisions and sins and to demonstrate the power of God's grace. Jesus reached across deeply held biases, prejudices, and other forms of human divisions as he ministered and delivered his message of God's grace and hope for the human community. The vision of a human community grounded in love and grace was central to the message that Jesus promoted as he addressed the human condition of hatred and brokenness in which he lived. For example, the story of the Good Samaritan was exactly such a message. Jesus' contacts with the poor and underclasses modeled the message of grace. Jesus provided glimpses of the beloved community in his work and teachings. He provided glimpses as he reached across social chasms of ethnicity, religion, and race to demonstrate not only God's grace but also how we are to live in the human community of love—the beloved community.

How do we continue the work that God mandated and that Jesus initiated? Are we called to identify, define, and confront human injustice, hatred, and disdain based on race and ethnicity? Are we to free people from fear, prejudice, and ignorance? Are we called to transform the human community into the beloved community? Is this the task of God's people of faith? We can begin with the theological task of naming racism a sin. As a sin, it is clearly against God's will and vision for humanity. As a sin, it calls all people who benefit, promote, or passively allow racism to oppress our fellow human beings to confess their sin and seek forgiveness. As the beloved community, we should all seek to be cleansed from this sin.

Signs of Hope

The call to The United Methodist Church to the task of building a beloved community is a sign of hope. It is a sign that our leadership has heard God's mandate; as a church, we have no choice but to heed that call. Our communities are broken along racial, ethnic, religious, political, and class lines. The church, as Christ's body, is called to model God's vision for a beloved community. There are glimpses of that vision within the church today. In the United States, the support for the National Plan for Hispanic/Latino Ministries is an important sign that provides hope and resources for ministry with this population. As an official project of the General Church, the National Plan is an important affirmation of the historic ministry with the Latino/Hispanic population, and also to the urgent necessity to strengthen our current efforts in light of population growth. The National Plan is a sign of hope that we are seeking to build the beloved community.

The development of plans for Hispanic ministries among annual conferences is a hopeful sign that the beloved community might be closer. To see conference coordinators for Hispanic ministries working with cabinets and bishops to address the presence of Latinos is a sign that the church is exploring how to engage Latinos in community and in the life of the church. Even more encouraging is to observe local congregations consider how they might reach out to Hispanics in their communities in spite of the anti-Hispanic and anti-immigrant sentiments. These efforts are glimpses that the beloved community may be possible.

Another sign of hope is that within the last generation four Latinos and Latinas have been elected to the office of bishop. We celebrate this accomplishment and affirmation. At the present time, only two bishops remain in active office after two bishops (Elias Galvan and Joel Martinez) have retired. Bishop Minerva Carcaño serves in California (Western Jurisdiction) and newly elected Bishop Cynthia Fierro Harvey serves in Louisiana (South Central Jurisdiction). We eagerly await such signs in all of the other United Methodist jurisdictions. In addition, across the nation we see the appointment of more Latinas and Latinos to key positions such as district superintendents and other positions within the leadership of the church as a sign of hope. The increase of cross-ethnic appointments is a significant indication that The United Methodist Church may indeed be open to and moving toward being a beloved community.

An important sign of hope is the presence of the Hispanic/Latino voice within the United Methodist community. MARCHA (Metodistas Asociados Representando la Causa Hispana Americana) is the voice of advocacy for Latinos and Latinas within the church. This is the voice that Latinos and Latinas have chosen to speak on behalf of their communities. The very existence of MARCHA is a sign of hope because it reflects the determination of Hispanics to be active and faithful members of The United Methodist Church. They care enough about the church and their communities to organize and give voice to their concerns and vision of what they expect from the beloved community. That the general church recognizes MARCHA as the official Hispanic caucus is truly a sign of hope.

The most compelling sign of hope is the Hispanic/Latino population itself. This population has overcome many social and cultural barriers to become Methodists and Protestants within their Catholic families and communities. They have paid huge personal and social prices to be members of The United Methodist Church. Their love for the church is unquestionable. They have experienced The United Methodist Church from days of segregation through trying days of social change. To join the Methodist church was not simply denominational switching. It involved personal and spiritual conversion. Their commitment to the church in spite of perceived and experienced prejudices and other obstacles will not diminish their resolve. Hispanic United Methodists are the greatest signs of hope.

Concluding Thoughts

We have had challenges and resolutions before. The church has a long history of calling itself to other challenges. For example, issues such as slavery, civil rights, and homosexuality have tested our resolve to be the faithful church as we struggle to be a beloved community. Yet, we are still the church as we seek to face yet another challenge. The commitment of The United Methodist Church to minister with Latinos and Hispanics will be tested by its own ability and willingness to embrace this population as a full member of the beloved community. To do so will require serious, truthful, and holistic reflection on racism within our United Methodist Church and our broader community. Without such transparency, the beloved community will continue to be simply a hopeful vision.

For Further Reading

González, Justo, ed. *Each in Our Own Tongue: A History of Hispanic United Methodism*. Nashville: Abingdon Press, 1991.
Barton, Paul. "Inter-Ethnic Relations between Mexican American and Anglo American Methodists in the U.S. Southwest 1836-1938," in *Protestantes/Protestants*. Nashville: Abingdon Press, 1999.

CHAPTER FOUR

Becoming Beloved Communities in Europe: A Challenge to Expand Our Comfort Zone

Åsa Nausner

Here is the room where all are equal,
tall and small,
women and men,
poor and rich.

Here before God we all are unique

in the church,
in the world.[1]

Lagom—a Swedish Vision

This liturgy is celebrated in an intercultural congregation in Northern Europe. It expresses the prophetic vision of the church as a place where we learn to practice equal relationships. It is a vision that nurtures my hope, strengthens my will, and guides my actions. "All are equal" means that everyone counts and that no one should be ignored into "nobodiness" in our communities.[2] This liturgy calls for a community where we view one another and our differences with the eyes of God as unique and precious. We need such liturgies to counter colonial fantasies, still lingering on the European continent, about the superiority of one group of people over other groups of people.

The heritage of the European nations' engagement in the colonial era, in Anti-Semitism and in Communist totalitarianism, still challenges ordinary people and politicians all over Europe. The colonial idea that the cultural or religious other is inferior to white Christian Europeans needs to be resisted over and over again. Against violence, hate, and marginalization, I believe we, as Christians, are called to deal with our prejudices and practice respect toward fellow human beings whether in the pews, on the streets, on the other side of the Atlantic, or beyond the equator.

As European communities become increasingly culturally diverse, we need religious and social visions of equality and justice. In my native language of Swedish, the word *lagom* implies just such a vision of equality. *Lagom* means sharing so that all may have enough: in the family, in society, and in the world. *Lagom* reminds me that I will be fine only when my neighbor is fine. The vision inherent in *lagom* implies that a good communal life must be lived in mutual respect with others. This word does not have an exact English equivalent, but can mean "enough, sufficient, adequate, or just right."[3] Often, *lagom* is explained in reference to the Vikings sharing beer in a horn, "laget om," among the team. *Lagom* in this case represents an equal distribution of food around the table. At its strongest, *lagom* is thus an ethical term, a guide to our use of resources.

Imagine harvest time at a farmer's house with the family and a lot of farm helpers around the table. When the dish of potatoes and meatballs is passed around, each person is supposed to adjust his or her serving in order for all the others to be satisfied as well. This image reminds us that we need to see and hear the needs of people in our societies in order to know how to share resources. *Lagom* is a simple vision for life, yet so difficult to put into daily practice. *Lagom* must be defined again and again, in every time and context. The beloved community for me is signified by just sharing of resources and open respectful communication about human pain, needs, and desires.

Unfortunately, *lagom* can have a second meaning as well. When we lose sight of the goal of equal and just sharing with the most vulnerable members of societies, it can suggest an attitude that prevents newness and transformation. When white Swedes[4] expect immigrants and strangers to behave in a certain way, *lagom* acquires a sense of behaving in accordance with traditional "Swedish" culture and the meaning of *lagom* as respect and equal sharing is lost. *Lagom* can thus imply that newcomers must assimilate into the larger society and become "Swedish." That one should not speak loudly in public places is but one example of such a Swedish norm. In this sense, *lagom* becomes a norm for the "insiders" to control "outsiders," and the notion of equality inherent in the word is transformed into a demand for sameness and assimilation. As with many good words and good intentions, lagom can be negatively transformed into something entirely different if we are not alert.

I begin my article with this reflection on lagom because it sheds light on the complexities of the struggle to envision, describe, and build beloved communities in Europe. There are many good intentions that have two sides, good for some but devastating for others. It is hard to admit that while my *lagom* community often sets out with good intentions, it simultaneously often harbors attitudes that build up walls and construct new borders that exclude members of minority groups and newcomers both in church and society.

I feel a need to reflect on what is good and to be open about what is destructive on my European home continent. As an educator, I am convinced that open, respectful, and critical constructive exchange across differences, exploring important human, religious, social, and political issues, is in itself a significant sign of the beloved community. The way in which we live is of social and spiritual concern. We express our longing for the beloved community when we practice respect for human dignity and live with a vision of justice. In this longing, we who are Christians are open to the Spirit of God who created us all equal and different. When we work together with people of good will from all walks of life, we envision the beloved community.

My Personal Journey

In what follows, I share personal experiences, offer a biblical reflection, and discuss the signs of longing for the beloved community I see in Europe today. In light of the continuing, everyday presence of ethnocentrism and racism, Martin Luther King's vision of "the beloved community" remains an urgent challenge for

European Christians. Many Europeans feel uncertain about their role in an increasingly pluralistic, intercultural, interreligious society. But I believe renewed attention to King's vision will give us courage to engage in relationships across cultural borders, and so to discover where God will meet us. Beloved community calls us to open our doors and our borders to newcomers, not to close them in their faces. Concretely, this means we are all called to participate in tearing down, brick by brick, the walls of silence, xenophobia, and racism in our communities and to envision new relationships across cultural and racial borders.

In order to be faithful to the task of reflecting on the beloved community, we must also look honestly at some instances where we have failed our vision. This is not meant to discourage us; rather, such critical self-reflection can stir our desire to participate in building good communities. By looking at examples of good relationships as well as reflecting on where we fail as communities, we can hope to expand our vision and hearing in order to make sure there is enough space, justice, and freedom for all.

By all I mean the diversity of migrants and non-migrants, women and men, black and white, people of Christian, Muslim, or other religions, as well as marginalized groups of people. We, the people of Europe, are people with different social experiences such as with or without experiences of war, with or without experiences of oppression; we are unemployed or employed, we are children, youth, and adults; further we are diverse in our sexual orientation, in our political affiliations, and in our eating habits.[5] Needless to say, there are many national histories, personal stories, and dreams to be told from the European continent. I cannot represent them all, but I can share some of my experiences and perspectives, primarily from Western Europe.[6]

Amidst all this European diversity, I am a white woman, born in Sweden in the early 1960s. I am an ecumenically spirited Christian, a Methodist who grew up in the Lutheran tradition with both Pentecostal and atheist relatives. With one grandmother Lutheran and the other Pentecostal, I learned about diversity in worship and theology among Christians early on and was inspired by how faith in God led each of my grandmothers to diaconal and mission activities. Their faith prompted action: they supported missionaries in Africa and regularly visited the sick and elderly in their communities.

I grew up with my mother, father, and younger brother in Sweden, a predominantly white and largely culturally homogeneous northern European nation.[7] Although the political and religious landscape has shifted through the years, Sweden is still shaped by social democratic and liberal democratic politics, and Lutheran Christianity remains the dominant religion. I grew up in a welfare society with a political will to share financial resources with children, women, the elderly, and the sick. By the 1970s, we already had state-run preschools, women's rights were to some extent protected by national policy, and we all took social health care and good retirement conditions for granted. Sweden welcomed many refugees.

The most significant sociopolitical transformations experienced on my continent during the last fifty years are: the end of the cold war era, with the fall of the wall between Eastern and Western Europe and not, least, increasing cultural, religious, and ethnic diversity. At times Swedes think about the previous "imagined" homogeneity as if there was a time when a Swede on a train could look around in the coach guessing what everyone was having for dinner, and be right about it. This is not the case anymore, if it ever was. Increasingly, Swedish social researchers and ethnographers challenge the myth of the previous "imagined" homogeneity of the welfare state. "Our culture has long been influenced by impulses from outside," state Daniel Andersson and Åke Sander, referring to the presence of central European peoples and of Jewish people for example.[8]

The intimate community of my childhood was not, at first glance, culturally diverse, but this quickly changed. The world entered my family. An uncle introduced a Turkish girlfriend, and two cousins were adopted from Ethiopia. I had a best friend whose father originated from (the former) Yugoslavia. One Finnish and two Indian students accompanied me through my first years of school. Some of my fellow Swedes thought, as I did, that the Indian students smelled strange; I guess they ate more garlic and other spices than we did at that time. This was enough to increase the distance that was already there between us due to language problems. Nevertheless, these early contacts spurred my interest in people from various cultures. Since then, I have been on a cross-cultural journey, personally and professionally.

Increasingly, I find myself reflecting on how my protected upbringing as a white West-European child influences my own commitment to the vision of beloved communities in an intercultural era. Already as a student in Lund and Uppsala, my worldview widened, I met international students, guests to the church from all over the world, and for some time I had Roma neighbors.[9] I did not talk much with my Roma neighbors, unfortunately, and I remember feeling very distant from this cultural group. My only connection to this community was a children's book about Katizi, a Roma girl.[10] I once asked my parents about their relationships to Roma and Sinti in Sweden—a conversation that taught me that Roma had a place in my family history, even if it was never spoken about.

My father grew up in a small village where, in the 1940s and 1950s, the Roma would arrive every summer with their tents and offer the people in the village services of various kinds, like cleaning copper pots. This is a particularly messy job, and the Swedish villagers were grateful for this service. However, it was not socially accepted for my father and his friends to develop any closer contact with the Roma youth. The youth in the village were not supposed to join the music and evening dances with the Roma. They could watch the fires and listen to the music only from a distance. The copper pot my parents later gave me reminds me of this distant connection with the Roma minority group that even today remains marginalized in Sweden and all over Europe.

I spent seven years of my professional life in the United States and an additional seven years in Germany. I have been working for many years as a director of Christian Education, and I currently teach courses in Communication, including a course in Intercultural Communication, at a Methodist School of Theology. On a daily basis, I seek to participate in building a community across differences: in the classroom, in the church, in the voting booth, and in my family. By critically following what is happening in the world around me, I learn to see the complexity of problems and am challenged to participate in seeking solutions. I know that Christ is present where I hesitate to go, calling me to walk with open eyes and ears.

The development and success of strong, healthy, diverse communities is, in my mind, an issue for all citizens. This urgent task cannot be left to European politicians, religious groups, and community leaders. It really matters how we treat and talk about one another around the kitchen table, in schools, churches, and marketplaces. Do we look at the intercultural transformation of our societies as a gift of God? Do we deny or lament this development?

Experiences from Christian Youth Groups

My family moved several times as I grew up. Even if it made me uncomfortable at first to approach new neighbors, I learned to enjoy meeting people in different places more than I feared it. It takes courage to meet new people even within your own cultural group. We do not connect automatically and are not always kind to one another. I knew about bullying from close friends. I have seen how discrimination for petty reasons, such as the wrong kind of glasses, can break a young person. I guess I have been lucky personally. In my various experiences with people, my worst fears never materialized. Over and over again, I was accepted in new schools, even if I had a different Swedish accent, which revealed that I had lived in another part of Sweden. It was for me a balance between keeping my self-respect and accepting that I had to adjust my accent in order to make friends.

The youth group in my local Lutheran congregation in Sweden was a nurturing community for me during my teens. It did me good to be welcomed and included by this group, even though I was not a "traditionally raised" Christian. I became involved when my best friend at school asked me to come along to meet other teens in the church. At first I hesitated, but agreed to try it out. I needed a loving community. For me, the church was a place of intense discussions, of Bible study, of planning and participating in worship services, and, last but not least, of trying to make a difference in the world through various projects, marches, and fundraising. The leaders of the congregation trusted us and counted on us. I do not know where I would be today without this experience.

In Swedish society, faith was and still is viewed as a private concern. Sweden counts as one of the most secularized nations in the world. The Lutheran church is the main denomination, but as a result of immigration, there is a growing presence of other Christian denominations as well as a range of religious groups, the largest being Islam. Growing up in a family with skeptical yet loyal views toward Christianity, it took time for me to figure out my relationship with God, Jesus Christ, and the Church. My father had negative experiences of Christians being coercive while speaking of love. This motivated me to take a closer look at those who call themselves Christians. My mother is an open and positive person. She always finds ways to speak to strangers and people she has never met before. Early on, I learned to observe what people did, to see whether they really meant what they said.

During my teenage years, Christians from various denominations fascinated me with their social engagement. The people who particularly impressed me were those who cared for "outsiders" in the society at large. Christian faith was revealed to me by people who helped one another survive, who comforted one another, who listened to one another, and who invited one another and newcomers into fellowship to be part of God's diverse family.

I encountered Swedish Christians who engaged with the homeless. During some years, my youth group participated in ecumenical Christmas parties with recovering alcoholics. I learned not to fear what might look strange, and I learned to see the individual underneath the surface. It felt as if something important united us across all our differences. We also learned about some of the social conditions contributing to alcoholism.

Several pastors and older teens impressed me with their engagement with prisoners, a nuclear-free world, and the end of apartheid in South Africa. These were big issues in the 1980s. The discussion of these world struggles in the church contrasted starkly with the silence about social issues at our kitchen table at home. Through the church, I learned to look at social and political issues with a sense that things could be changed. What we did as individuals in our small town mattered. Later I learned about the butterfly effect, that a butterfly flapping her wings in Asia may cause a storm in the Americas.

Meeting black South Africans marked by the brutality of the apartheid regime became a turning point for me in terms of international, racial, and social awareness. As a teenager, I understood that human suffering must be an urgent concern for all Christians.

The violence invading some communities and the pain endured was beyond any logic and not to be ignored. It was through the South African perspective that the history of colonialism, slavery, and apartheid became tangible to me, and I started to realize how connected my life was with world history and, for example, the neocolonial trade of fruit.

When the South African guests asked us, white Swedish teenagers, how it was to live in freedom, we found few words to describe it. Strangely, it was as if we did not know that we lived in freedom, even though we had the right to speak up against injustices and despite the fact that there were no obstacles to arranging meetings, campaigns, or parties. This discussion with the South Africans made us feel that we were being too passive regarding justice issues. Did we really utilize our freedom well enough? I still feel challenged by this question from the black South Africans. How are we Christians in the West utilizing our freedom? What is God calling us to do with it?

I found passionate people in my local congregation committed to participate in changing the world for the better. They believed in a God of transformation and so I started to as well. The church opened a door to the world for me, a door that cannot be closed and must not be closed. I met God the same time I discovered social injustice and the needs of people in this world. For me, the church became a meeting point of diverse local and international people, a kind of open house where all at some time had been newcomers. Primarily, my youth group became a good community where I was challenged to be aware of what was happening beyond my little town. We started to boycott fruit from South Africa, for example. Maybe, I was naïve back then, but in that case, I am still naïve. It is still my life's focus to seek signs of God's transformative power in people and in communities.

A Stranger in Europe

Another story illustrates that there is still much to be done to build good communities in Europe. Strolling with an African American friend through my city one summer opened my eyes to the subtle discrimination of strangers in my community. This walk through my central European city full of historical sites, lush gardens, and beautiful churches usually gives my visitors a sense of charm. At one of the ice-cream parlors, we usually enjoy the golden summer weather and talk about the privilege of being on vacation. This time it was different.

I took my African American friend on my usual tour for guests. The sun was shining, and we ate lunch at a restaurant on a side street close to the market place. We window shopped, visited the main church, and talked about common friends. As our walk was coming to an end, we stopped in front of a bookstore, and my friend asked me if I had noticed a person following us. She pointed toward an ordinary looking white European man probably in his forties or so some steps behind us. No, I had not seen him before.

"You know," my friend said, upset, "he walked by us as we were eating lunch, and I knew that he noticed me. Later as we came out from the church, he walked by us again while saying something that I couldn't understand. Now here he is again. It makes me uncomfortable, and I cannot but think that it is 'racial.' I do not think he wants me here. In his eyes, I don't belong."

The usual peaceful enjoyment of European culture did not happen during this city tour. The charm evaporated, and we had no desire to stop at any ice-cream parlor anymore. I learned that as a white European woman, I could not always sense the presence of racism right in the middle of my own community. It is hard to acknowledge that the place where I, as a white person, feel protected and at home, can be so unfriendly toward someone who is non-white and appears non-European. I experienced the hard way what it is to belong to the norm group, and that my community is not a good place for all.

The story above is not a single occurrence. Shneur Kesselman, who has been serving as the Jewish Rabbi in Malmö in southern Sweden for the last seven years, shares similar experiences, and he is not alone. "I was not prepared for the hate I was to meet," he says, describing the anti-Semitism directed toward him and his children on the streets of one of the most multicultural cities in Sweden. "The words and the fact that people spit at me is uncomfortable. But what scares me the most is the hate that can be seen in the eyes of the people, in the eyes of the people who want evil. I have no idea where their limit is, how far they can go."[11] In the year 2011 alone, 5,140 hate crimes were reported in Sweden, half of which had anti-religious motives, predominantly against Jews and Muslims.

Churches, and especially the growing number of intercultural congregations, in Europe have to adjust to the situation of hostility toward people who do not look European or speak the national language well. A German pastor I interviewed reports that many of her church members daily experience subtle or overt racism in the streets of her city. "Our immigrant members have learned to be careful; they do not like to go outside after dark because they know that violence could happen anywhere." At big festivals in the city where alcohol is served, racism more often shows its ugly face, according to this pastor. Therefore, she avoids planning church meetings during these festivals, so that black people and migrants can avoid the city center.

Sacred Encounters

I was hungry and you gave me food, I was thirsty and you gave me something to drink, I was a stranger and you welcomed me, I was naked and you gave me clothing, I was sick and you took care of me, I was in prison and you visited me. (Matt. 25:35-36)

According to Matthew 25, we encounter Jesus Christ in people whom we categorize as not belonging to "us"—people at the margins of our societies—in the prisons, hospitals, and homes for asylum seekers. Unfortunately, not all who hear Jesus' words understand this point. We learn from the parable that some are shocked to discover that we can serve God among the strangers and marginalized. For many, whether in biblical times or today, the margins of societies are filled with problems, sadness, and dirt. Nothing good is expected from there. But through these verses we understand that sacred encounters take place on the borders of our societies.

Questions trouble the minds of those who thought of themselves as righteous in this text: "When did we see you hungry?" and "Were you a stranger?" We can hear shame in these voices. Jesus often shares a parable to help those listening to think outside the box. His stories often provoke established people to change their thinking and social behavior. Is this story his way to awaken our consciousness? Is this text calling established people to awareness about the reality of people we have learned to exclude?

I am reading this text at a time when media all over Europe report about ongoing hostility and racism against black people and against the Roma and Sinti peoples. I read about overfilled temporary homes for asylum seekers, increased unemployment for immigrants due to the economic crisis, and the rising number of undocumented refugees in prison along the European borders. All over Europe, there are refugees and immigrants who inhabit the margins where poverty, thirst, and hunger abound.

Many immigrants in Europe still struggle to gain entrance, acquire permission to stay and work, and to connect with the culture around them. Eyal Sharon Krafft is an Israeli-born journalist who writes about his experiences as a "culturally different" immigrant to Sweden. To him, the silence he experienced in Sweden was like a wall:

"How I hate this silence! It surrounds me like an invisible wall against the world. A world which is imbued by Swedishness. A world which is impregnable. Provokingly inaccessible. I am and remain foreign. The silence makes sure I do."[12]

Krafft continues to explore the silence he experienced from the Swedish norm culture: from my fellow Swedish citizens, or maybe he is even talking about me. "You are so silent that I hear my breath when meeting you with my straight forward gaze as I walk down the busy street in the city center."[13] While silence is a precondition to being open to hear the stranger, it can also become a tool of segregation. We need to notice where silence hinders communication in order to break that silence.

Reading the text of Matthew 25, I discover how Jesus challenges the ignorance and the excluding silence of the people in the dominant "norm-society" of his time. People in the center of any society are the ones who formulate and set the normative ethical ideas of what is right and wrong in any culture. The dominant group consists of people who are not poor, not in prison, and definitely not strangers. Being busy with their daily lives, jobs, and children, people in a norm-group often have neither the time nor the motivation to leave their safety zones. Men and women in any norm-group have learned to think of a good life in terms of being materially and legally secure. They feel that they can influence their society through political activity and elections. When we feel that the social institutions where we live are there for us, in support for our problems and concerns, we belong to a norm-group. Jesus challenges this perspective. Can we see what those who are not safe among us need?

People in a norm-group do not necessarily think of themselves in terms of any cultural identity. If you belong to a norm-group in any European nation, it means that despite the increasing reality of ethnic diversity within nations, you are most often viewed by others as a "national," or as "white." If you belong to the norm group, most probably other people in this group can easily and correctly pronounce your name, and you are not looked down on for the way you look, speak, or dress. Further, you are not asked on the streets for your passport or your legal papers. In short: you don't stand out. To be accepted as belonging to the norm means to be viewed as a "normal" citizen. It includes social and cultural status and privilege. Social and cultural status is often based on economic privilege, but not always. A person can be privileged based on nationality, culture, or religion as well as based on language skills or physical appearance.

Social and psychological reports prove that it is hard for a person of a norm-group to empathize with people in other groups. It demands courage; it can be risky, but one can also learn a lot. "In-group–out-group" dynamics is a psychological theory that explains why and how people define their own social, cultural, or ethnic groups in positive terms in contrast to other cultural/ethnic groups, whom they then describe in negative terms as different and often dangerous.

The Matthew text is subtitled "The Final Judgment" in my Bible. However, in these words I find an ethical model for a new beginning toward the survival, flourishing, and common future for all, starting at the margins. This text is a good ethical base for building a good community. The God we meet in the Greek Testament is a God who can be found among the poor, the stranger, and the sick. This text provokes me to dream of and work for a European future where strangers are not left hungry, sick, and excluded.

Fear of Diversity

Despite often-expressed good intentions, there is a lack of political will to protect those who are different from the dominant norm group. We must admit that the fortress of Europe is still in construction. New political parties with a nationalistic agenda in many countries all over Europe argue that immigration is the main threat to welfare and security for the national norm groups. Daily acts of discrimination are forcing non-Europeans, refugees, immigrants of various heritage, and minorities to be on their guard in the schools, the workplaces, and in the public sphere.

The myth that societies in Europe are being threatened by immigration can motivate violent acts, as we have seen in Norway and Germany in 2011. Through these experiences, people in Europe have learned that "the terrorist" is not always a stranger; he or she can be one of "us." Many people in Europe are still in shock over what happened in Oslo, Norway, during the summer of 2011. A single, white Norwegian man was determined (from his perspective) that Norway needed to be "rescued" from becoming increasingly multicultural. His vision led him to plan two murderous attacks, which he carried out on July 22. By bombing the Norwegian Government in the city center of Oslo and then by killing youth on a political youth camp on the island Utøya, this man intentionally targeted people who were working for a vision of a multicultural Norway.[14]

The Oslo tragedy seemed to be motivated by fear of a future of cultural diversity, similar to what motivates the underground "neo-Nazi trio," so far identified as two men and one woman, all three white and German. As the mysterious murders of nine immigrant shopkeepers and one German policewoman during the years 2000–2007 were revealed to have been carried out by this neo-Nazi group, Germany stood in shock. Angela Merkel deemed these acts an attack on democracy, declaring: "We are determined to defend our open and tolerant way of life against horrid criminals and their despicable ideology."[15] In response to these incidents, famous musicians have given concerts to protest neo-Nazi ideology, and marches against racism have been organized in many places all over Germany.

These violent examples tell me that something is radically problematic in our democratic societies. Discrimination and racism are still alive, leading to segregation, violence, and death on the European continent. This tells me that we have not been dealing enough with the history of colonialism and the development of Europe, which, to a large extent, involved unjust and violent relationships with people of different cultures and religions, within Europe and globally.

A Political Campaign

Cold winds and harsh words against minorities and immigrants are felt throughout Europe. The traditionally marginalized groups of Roma and Sinti suffer from double-standard legal procedures in France, but not only there. They are literally being kicked out of some western European nations. Their houses are being destroyed, and they are forced to wander around in Europe. Political parties like the "Sweden Democrats" in Sweden distribute propaganda suggesting that life would be better without non-European migrants.

Switzerland is but one other example. In the fall of 2011, a poster for the People's Party (SVP) in Switzerland read, "Kick them out." This simple message was printed next to an image of sheep on the national flag, a red flag marked with a white cross. The poster shows one black sheep being literally kicked out of the flag by a white sheep; two other white sheep look on, seemingly approving the bullying going on in the picture. The symbolism could not be more drastic. Many refer to immigrants as the "black sheep" in today's Switzerland. The generalization in this image is brutal. The idealization of the white norm-group as pure and superior (the white sheep) masks the cruelty of their stance, while the negative characterization of the other (the black sheep) encourages segregation, separation, and hate.

In 2011, about 22 percent of the 7.4 million inhabitants in Switzerland were people with an immigrant background. Immigrant is classified as a person with at least one parent born outside Switzerland. Italians, Germans, and Portuguese also have a long history of immigration to Switzerland. While some West European immigrants have successfully integrated, more recent immigrants from the Balkans or from African states are met with reluctance and fear. New politicians are quick to employ catchy and emotional messages. "Kick them out" is reverberating all over Europe. I recently saw the same symbolism on a Swedish blue and yellow flag. People from all over the world have lived in Sweden and other European nations for generations; nevertheless, immigrants still end up as strangers at the bottom of the social pecking order in most European societies.

Many Faces of Migration

Despite increased work on immigration policy in several nation states and in many EU institutions, including organizations in the civil society and religious organizations, the list of segregating, marginalizing, and excluding forces that daily confront people of non-European origin is long and disturbing. A human disaster and refugee scandal is taking place at the borders between Europe and North Africa. To enter any EU nation legally, one needs to apply for a visa, which is almost impossible for a refugee to receive. Most refugees therefore take huge risks in order to reach the European mainland. Not until someone is inside the border can the process of applying for asylum start. However, the borders to Europe are increasingly becoming a death zone:

> For many, it is their last journey. Annually, hundreds of men, women, and children are dying at the gates of Europe. They freeze to death as they attempt to swim through border floods; they lose their lives in the minefields of the Greek-Turkish border, or suffocate in containers on the roads. People drown almost daily on their way to Europe in the Mediterranean.[16]

Laws and legal status on immigration, as well as popular terminology, have changed over the years. Even after an immigrant's papers are cleared, the negotiation of identity takes many turns. Turkish immigrants in Germany often explain how their identity has been defined in different terms during the last fifty years; the first generation "immigrants" were called guest workers, then it changed to Turks, and during the last years, most Turkish immigrants in Germany are viewed in religious terms, as Muslims. Increasingly, people of Turkish immigrant heritage in Germany refuse to be defined as either Turkish or German, but want to retain both cultural identities, which is slowly becoming socially accepted.

In the U.S., citizenship is often marked with a hyphen. In Europe, there is no similar tradition. Each European nation has been viewed as "home" for a certain national group that ties its genealogy to a specific place. Strangers are met with hostility. Although immigrants have long contributed significantly to national developments, they have most often been marginalized.

Immigration in Europe has many faces. On the one hand, most nations need immigrants to improve their negative population curve, yet immigrants and refugees are often seen as a problem by many political parties. It is almost impossible for a person born outside Europe to be accepted as a European, even with a European passport. In 2011, a Swedish newspaper presented a range of facts regarding immigration in Sweden. One article reported a new ethnic dimension of poverty. It is immigrants in Sweden who are at the greatest risk of losing their jobs as the financial crisis continues.[17]

On the other hand, the same newspaper published an article titled, "Sweden would come to a halt without immigrants." In it, we learn that the presence of immigrants in certain jobs in Sweden is significant. For example, 36 percent of the bakers, 32 percent of the cleaning staff in hotels, and 24 percent of the drivers of buses and subway trains in Sweden have an immigrant background.[18] The hospitals would collapse without foreign workers, according to the same article. In Stockholm, the capital of Sweden, 30 percent of the doctors in hospitals were not born in Sweden, and half of these were born outside the EU.

At the same time, there are people working hard for human rights within Europe. There are many institutional initiatives and voluntary organizations working against restrictive refugee policies in Europe.[19] There are initiatives for diversity management in the social and business sectors. When a racist crime is made known, people often take to the streets to demonstrate against racism and xenophobia in their villages, towns, or cities. Racist crimes are increasingly appearing in court.

Intercultural Congregations

As a European Christian, I am always on the lookout for examples of courage and creativity in counteracting prejudice and discrimination. I have learned a lot about strategies to fight racism from observing intercultural dynamics of professional soccer, from the initiatives of various NGOs, and from faith communities. What we need is individual and professional commitment to non-discriminatory relationships in politics, among NGOs, in sports, and in churches. We urgently need to reflect on and learn from experiences of relationships across cultural diversity in our communities. The growing number of culturally diverse congregations in Europe also offers such places of learning. Intercultural congregations are contact zones when it comes to living in diversity.

Being a United Methodist in Europe means in some way being a Christian on the margin, The UMC is a small denomination compared to the larger Evangelical Lutheran, Catholic, and Orthodox churches. Methodist immigrants and transnational professionals continue to make up a significant part of the UMC in Europe. This has been a historical trend. In the nineteenth century, many of the Methodist churches in Europe were comprised of migrating peoples. In twentieth-century Austria, it was, to a large extent, refugees from Eastern Europe and migrants from the United States who helped to rebuild the Methodist church after WWII. In the nineteenth century, it was British workers in Stockholm who made up the first Methodist congregations. While other Methodist congregations in Europe historically have been comprised of people of the national norm group, we are currently witnessing a steady rise of intercultural and international congregations within our denomination.[20]

In Germany, we find several congregations made up primarily of one migrant group worshiping in their language of origin. A wide spectrum of language groups are represented; including English, Korean, Vietnamese, and Twi, a language spoken in Ghana.[21] I have met British Methodists from Ghana now living in Britain who are actively supporting development programs such as schools and agricultural programs in their home villages. This congregation also organizes cross-cultural trips in order for teens from Ghanaian families living in England and teens from white British families to learn about Ghanaian life and spirituality. Immigrants thus cannot be generalized as passive; they are agents of social change in their countries of origin and in their new homelands.

Congregations are increasingly becoming meeting places across cultural borders. For example, in one traditionally white congregation members reach out to immigrant children on a playground next to the church. Playing with kids from various cultures has, in this case, contributed to breaking habits of harassment and fighting on this playground. It has also given this congregation new cross-cultural and interreligious contacts and coworkers in the ministry for children and youth. This is but one example of what it means to be a church in an intercultural society.

"Suddenly, people just came to us," a Scandinavian pastor tells me. Amazed that Christian immigrants and refugees found their way to this small congregation, this pastor started on a journey learning to live and worship with people she first viewed as strangers. She states it simply: "We meet across cultural and social borders every Sunday, and thereby we practice a model of life. We learn to live in diversity as the way it should be. It is the Kingdom of God." This does not mean that living with diversity is always an easy or uncomplicated road to travel.

Two young African students share that they finally found their second home in this small congregation. First engaged in the youth work, they then joined the worship group, excited to help out with the Holy Communion. "Maybe some Swedes were skeptical of the honest commitment of these youth at the beginning," the pastor tells me, "but now the African teens are both known as the individuals they are, by their names, and we cherish each other more and more." However, this pastor acknowledges that she needs new communication skills in order to facilitate cooperation among members from various cultures. "It is not always easy, and some members are more suspicious to newcomers than others and do not want the pastor to spend all her time with them."

Several highly intercultural congregations are learning to practice a broad and active form of networking within the congregation as well as with people in other institutions in the civil society. The pastor in Sweden continues: "Once a Kenyan member brought another pregnant African woman to our Sunday morning worship, to see if we could help her." With some experience now, this pastor has adopted new roles and widened networks since the immigrants arrived. "That morning, I quickly knew that I needed to find a gynecologist and a lawyer, and I did. I am in contact with resource persons ecumenically who know more than I do about immigration. I have a list of people, organizations, and institutions to call when I feel overloaded."

This pastor is aware of her limitations and shares that she is impressed by how immigrant women often help other immigrants or refuges. As studies have shown, integration is a process involving various steps. Often new immigrants are first integrated in a group of other immigrants, then follows integration into the larger society, connecting with nationals, learning the language, and finding employment. For the second step, openness on the part of European citizens is required. Integration is a mutual process.

Personal experiences of being a stranger, of traveling, or of living abroad might help national citizens to open up toward newcomers. "Many Germans have no idea of the complexity involved in starting a new life in a new country," the German pastor of an international congregation tells me. She is keen to say that we should not take people's resistance or critique too negatively.

For me, this means that it is very hard for some people to go beyond their comfort zone. There is a saying from where I come from; "what the farmer doesn't know, he doesn't eat." It means that we don't need to try new things, and even more so, it means that you often avoid trying new things. However, I believe God is calling us out of our comfort zone.

This congregation in Germany is doing its part to shape a new vision of interracial, intercultural community, a vision that creates a stark contrast to the Swiss poster with the black sheep ("Kick them out."). "Our congregation seeks to offer a place of safety for foreigners struggling to live and work in Germany," the pastor tells me. This Methodist congregation has a long history of welcoming diverse people. I meet families here; I meet single mothers, mixed-race couples, and people from all walks of life. It seems as if diversity is comfortable here. A significant number of ex-patriots from Britain, America, and Australia, as well as Germans are also devoted members. "Here, no one is asking questions. Here I can come as I am; I do not have to put on a face," says a white German woman.

I am convinced that diversity is something we must practice and learn again and again. It is not always smooth and fun; it is also challenging and frustrating at times. As the congregation's members, friends, and guests wrestle with the many practical challenges of diversity, questions of faith and culture become more urgent. Meeting immigrants in distress pushes members to be courageous. The pastor is currently guided by one question, and she is referring to Matthew 25: "What is Jesus asking us to do? When he says 'to feed the hungry,' what does it mean?" For the leaders as well as the pastor of this congregation, it is important to live deeply connected with the biblical message. They are carried by the experience of being coworkers with God in serving the poor and the stranger today.

For the pastor, it is critical to be involved for change. "We are called to contribute to change, with the sense that we can change things, we always have something to do." Together, the Church Council on Ministries identified children's needs as core to their calling in ministry and started there. The pastor explains:

> By offering homework support for asylum seekers and immigrant children and youth, we offer nourishment for the future. We are just helping our co-citizens a little bit to come along so they can better participate and help us build this city and this nation where we now live. For me, food is more than what you eat, it is to have homework support, it is essential for your future. It is food for a day so you can go on with your life.

I discover people in this congregation with the courage to speak up for the asylum seekers; whether working men, pregnant women, or children. For this congregation, the work of the church also includes visits and letters to social workers, embassies, and lawyers in support of immigrants and asylum seekers from this congregation. Laypeople and pastors have gained a special insight into how national policies and procedures for immigrants and refugees function in practice. They have seen good and bad. This pastor has become more skeptical about the national structure, as she has witnessed asylum seekers being denied care and basic dignity. Many fall through the cracks. "For example, in the summer, when the social worker goes on vacation, the weekly pay of pocket money for asylum seekers is not paid. It is hard to see people who so much depend on this sum to have to wait and get it retrospectively."

We still have a lot to learn and issues to discuss when it comes to achieving diversity among the leadership in international congregations, integrating a range of worship styles and theologies, and increasing the diversity of students and professors in theological education. The church is not immune to racism or xenophobia. Together with the German pastor, however, I am convinced that we need to build for the future, "Let us be honest, we know that Europe needs immigrants. For a common good future we need to make today as good as we can. In 30–40 years the immigrant kids on the streets will be pillars of our communities. We are here together." I envision most congregations in the future to be open to diversity.

Moving Forward

I have presented some problems and signs of promises from intercultural communities in Europe. We need more open discussions about this in the time to come, even if it involves conflicts about the interpretations of social needs in our communities.

We should not underestimate the transformative power of being in community with one another across cultural, social, and religious borders. It is always harder to build up than to tear down buildings as well as trust. The shortest definition of empathy I know is to "be there."[22] When we are present with one another, when we stand face to face, with our differences and similarities, we will find the way forward. Every encounter matters. When we listen actively without manipulation to the diverse and to the marginalized voices among us, we are living a vision of hope. We might then glimpse Christ. My vision of the beloved community is dynamic and not static.

I close with the sending words of the same liturgy from Scandinavia with which I started this article.

Now we go forth with open eyes
to reveal the inhumane
to fight for justice
and to discover You

in every person
carried by Your grace.[23]

Notes

1. Opening words of a liturgy by Thomas Kazen, professor of Theology at the Stockholm School of Theology in Sweden. The text in Swedish reads "Här är rummet där alla är lika: stora och små, kvinnor och män, fattiga och rika. Här inför Gud är alla unika i kyrkan, i världen" (translated into English by Åsa Nausner and Thomas Kazen). Used by permission.

2. Martin Luther King Jr. uses this term nobodiness in his "Letter from Birmingham Jail" (1963) in *The Essential Writings and Speeches of Martin Luther King, Jr.,* edited by James M. Washington (San Francisco: HarperCollins, 1986), 293.

3. See: www.en.wikipedia.org/wiki/lagom for more information and references.

4. I am using the term "white Swedish" to mark a citizen with a long genealogy in Sweden, meaning a citizen born in Sweden of white parents who were also born in Sweden. White skin color, however, does not automatically provide privilege in Europe; a white immigrant from Russia, South Africa, or the U.S. might be discriminated against in Sweden and Germany based on being a stranger, not knowing the cultural codes, or other markers such as limited language skills, dress codes, or religious symbols. I avoid the term "native Swedish," since it refers to the native indigenous population of the Sami people predominantly inhabiting Northern Scandinavia.

5. The continent of Europe has a population roughly 800 million people distributed among 49 sovereign nations. Only 27 of these nations are members of the European Union (EU). The EU member states are: Austria, Belgium, Bulgaria, Cyprus, Czech Republic, Denmark, Estonia, Finland, France, Germany, Greece, Hungary, Ireland, Italy, Latvia, Lithuania, Luxemburg, Malta, Netherlands, Poland, Portugal, Romania, Slovakia, Slovenia, Spain, Sweden, and the United Kingdom. Candidate countries to the EU: Croatia, Former Yugoslav Republic of Macedonia, Iceland, Montenegro, and Turkey. European Countries. States not in the EU: Albania, Andorra, Armenia, Azerbaijan, Belarus, Bosnia and Herzegovina, Georgia, Liechtenstein, Moldova, Monaco, Norway, Russia, San Marino, Serbia, Switzerland, Ukraine, and the Vatican City. For further information see: www.europa.eu/countries/index.

6. More than thirty European languages are spoken across Europe. Immigrants make up an average of 20 percent of the European population. There are public schools in larger cities where as many as 60 international languages are spoken. In Germany, most applications for asylum are currently submitted by refugees from Afghanistan, Iraq, and Iran. Find more facts on immigration in Germany (in German) under: www.proasyl.de.

7. Sweden is roughly the size of California, but it is populated by only 9 million citizens (compared to California's 38 million.)

8. Daniel Anderson and Åke Sander (eds.) in "Det mångreligiösa Sverige, ett landskap i förändring," [Translation of the title: "The multireligious Sweden, a landscape in transformation"] (Lund: Studentlitteratur, 2009), 28.

9. For more about the Roma and Sinti population in Europe see: www.osce.org/odihr/roma and www.stiftung-evz.de/eng/. Roma means human being in the Roma language, Sinti is another group.

10. The author Katarina Taikon (1932–1995) wrote children's books on the Roma culture for children and youth in Sweden starting in the 1960s. Taikon's books focus on the life and adventures of the young girl Katizi.

11. See www.dn.se/insidan-hem/jag-var-oforberedd-pa-det-hat-som-skulle-mota-mig. "Jag var oförberedd på det hat som skulle möta mig" ["I was not prepared for the hate that I was to encounter"] in *Dagens Nyheter* [*Daily News*] published 11/7/11.

12. Eyal Sharon Krafft, in the article "Tystnadens onda cirkel" ["The evil circle of silence"], in the anthology *Tyst [Silence]* (Stockholm: Verbum, 2004), 69).

13. Ibid.

14. "Oslo Bombings and Utoya Attack" in *The New York Times*, see: http://topics.nytimes.com/top/news/international/countriesandterritories/norway/index.html.

15. News Daily, "Merkel says neo-Nazi killings damage Germany's image" by Erik Kirschbaum, 11/23/11. www.newsdaily.com.

16. "Sterben auf der Flucht," [*"Dying while Fleeing"*] at www.proasyl.de, November 2011. (author's translation from German to English). See also the article "One survivor, 54 die at sea attempting the voyage to Italy from Libya,"10 July, 2012, under www.unhcr.org /4ffc59e89.html.

17. See the article, "Utrikesfödda har blivit största gruppen fattiga," ("Foreign born have become the largest group of the poor" by Lasse Granestrand, 12/2/11, *Dagens Nyheter*, 12/2/11, www.dn.se.

18. See the article "Utan invandrare stannar Sverige" (in translation: "Sweden would come to a halt without immigrants") by Lasse Granestrand, *Dagens Nyheter*, 12/4/11, www.dn.se.

19. See for example this German activist group, kein Mensch ist Illegal, meaning: no person is illegal, www.kmii.de.

20. See more information on The UMC in Europe on www.umc-europe.org, and www.emk.de . The UMC in Germany counts about 55,000 members and friends. The UMC in Central and Southern Europe is a relatively small church, which consists of 32,000 members and friends, spread over 16 nations, with more than 20 official languages. In Sweden, The United Methodist church recently joined the Baptist Union and the Mission Covenant Church in a new denomination, named Common Future.

21. See Carol Seckel, *Then let us no longer be strangers, diversity in the church*, D.Min thesis at Wesley Theological Seminary, May 2011.

22. Rosenberg discusses the meaning of empathy with philosophers like Martin Buber, Simone Weil, and Chuang Tzu in Marshall Rosenberg, *Gewaltfreie Kommunikation*, Paderborn: Junfermann Verlag, 2009, 113–115. This is the German translation of Marshall Rosenberg, *Non-Violent Communication: A Language of Life*, 2002.

23. Sending words from a liturgy, written by Thomas Kazen, professor in Theology at the Stockholm School of Theology in Sweden. In original language: "Nu går vi ut med öppna ögon, för att avslöja omänskligheten, kämpa för rätten, och upptäcka dig i varje medmänniska, burna av din nåd " (Translation into English by Åsa Nausner and Thomas Kazen). Used by permission.

For Further Reading

Streiff, Patrick. *Methodism in Europe: 19th and 20th Century*. Baltic Methodist Theological Seminary, 2003. [Streiff is the United Methodist Bishop of Central and Southern Europe.]

CHAPTER FIVE

New Eyes to See

Elaine A. Robinson

I was born in Pittsburgh, Pennsylvania, the daughter of a third-generation Latvian Jewish father and a second-generation Ukrainian Orthodox mother. We spoke no Yiddish or Ukrainian in our home, though we did eat bagels and lox—as well as other Eastern European delicacies such as matzo, kreplach, and blintzes—before it became fashionable. My family practiced no religious tradition, as both of my parents had abandoned the faith of their childhoods long before they married. When I was eight or nine years old, my father legally changed our "Jewish-sounding" family name so we would no longer have to defend a religion we did not practice. To this day, I have no great affinity for my surname, which says little about who I really am as it conjures up white, Anglo-Saxon Protestant heritage. And for the most part, I understood myself to be just a middle-class American. In short, as a white American, I did not have to think about race as I lived comfortably among the majority culture of the United States and encountered people of color mostly through the media and its portrayals.

When the mandated integration of public schools occurred in the early 1970s, for the first time in my life I came into regular contact with people of color. My parents, who were good secular humanists, taught us that "all people are the same," and I approached my new classmates with this simple belief that we were the same. Of course, I recognized that we were different in some ways, but as pre-teens none of us had been fully enculturated in the patterns of our racial groups. We hadn't yet learned the depths of racial discrimination and even hatred, such that at recess we could line up our volleyball teams according to color, using racial epithets as our team names and even considering them funny. My team, the white girls, was known as the "honkies." I suspect the children of color already had an inkling of the disparities that existed, as well as the painful racist history of the United States, even if I was largely ignorant. I did not yet grasp what it meant that some of my classmates spoke different languages at home; lived in neighborhoods quite distinct from my split-level, suburban existence; and held worldviews that did not mirror my own. Nor could I understand deeper levels of racial and cultural difference that existed. I just assumed everyone else was a lot like me, though with darker skin. To be fair, as Paul wrote to the Corinthians, "When I was a child, I spoke like a child, I thought like a child, I reasoned like a child" (1 Cor. 13:11).

As I grew, life placed me on my own Damascus Road where experiences and encounters and the Spirit of God could give me new eyes to see. Over my fifty some years, I've never lived for more than eight years in any one place. I've lived in Florida, Canada, Indiana, California, Colorado, Delaware, Ohio, Korea, Texas, Georgia, and Oklahoma. I've traveled and sometimes taught for days or weeks in Egypt, Israel, Argentina, Costa Rica, Cuba, Ivory Coast, the Philippines, Thailand, Russia, England, Germany, Spain, Italy, Switzerland, Austria, and France. The more time I've spent in different states, countries and cultures, the more I've begun to accept that people live in noticeably different ways within the United States and around the globe. Not only are there obvious differences in foods and languages, but deeper differences related to ways of learning, communicating, mourning, celebrating, and being a community.

But it wasn't until I was formed in the Christian faith and developed a sound theological understanding that I began to see the complexity of God's people in the tension of commonality and difference. Some ten or fifteen years ago, as a Christian, a clergyperson, and a theologically educated adult, I began to wrestle with the commonalities and differences among and within racial and ethnic communities, and I began to see white Americans as a racial group with ethnic and cultural differences and similarities. Sometimes white Americans view everyone else as being of a racial group, but not themselves, except when checking the "Caucasian" box on a government form. Race, of course, is truly only skin deep, as human beings are virtually identical biologically,[1] and the greatest differentiation genetically lies within racial groupings, not between them.

Ironically, after I confessed faith in Jesus Christ as an adult, faith in the One who came to offer life abundant to all people, I discovered many Christian churches don't seem to be any more informed than my secular parents were when it comes to the complexity of the human creature. Some churches seem even less willing than my secular parents were to embrace those who are of different races. I remember being invited to teach a Sunday school class at a large United Methodist, majority culture church. When the class leader, a white man, got up to pray and introduce me as the guest speaker to the all-white group, he began with a joke: "How do we know that Jesus was black? Because he loved gospel, called everyone brother, and couldn't get a fair shake." It was a racist moment. There is no other way to describe it, though I have little doubt he would say he meant no harm and loves everyone. I'm not sure what other members of the class thought, but because I was a guest, I said nothing. I should have begun my talk with a gentle and honest response to his joke, but I chose to remain silent. That silence made me complicit. I slipped comfortably into my white privilege as if it had never occurred.

New Eyes to See White Privilege

Since becoming a Christian in 1988, my eyes have been opened to see the presence of "white privilege" and the ways in which white culture determines the "standards" for how we should live, act, worship, and communicate in the United States. I believe in the depths of my heart that my awareness is a gift and a calling given to me by God. While there are many "book" definitions of white privilege, the basic idea is that in the United States, people who are thought to be white, Caucasian, Euro- or Anglo-American—whether they are white or can "pass" for white—have always had access to certain social, economic, and political benefits that are not easily obtained by persons of color. Of course there are impoverished white Americans who do not enjoy the opportunities available to middle-class and upper-class persons. Of course there are also persons of color who are wildly wealthy. But historically down through the present day, white persons in the United States have had advantages that others don't have, even though whiteness is socially-constructed, not biologically based. In fact, many persons who today are considered white Americans come from ethnic groups that were not thought to be "white" when they arrived in the United States, such as Italian and Irish immigrants.[2] They understood that being considered white would provide them with access to distinct benefits.

Some years ago, Peggy McIntosh wrote an essay entitled, "White Privilege: Unpacking the Invisible Knapsack," in which she listed examples of white privilege.[3] Some of the examples are serious; some, on the surface, are more trivial. But they help us to see how being white in the United States has its advantages. For example, schools routinely teach about white Americans, but less often about persons of color. What if the history of the United States were told through the eyes of American Indians? Would we still celebrate Columbus Day? White Americans are more apt to receive mortgages than equally qualified persons of color, more apt to be assisted by store salespersons than followed surreptitiously, and more apt to be ignored by police officers who will stop others for "driving while black or Latino." And, quite obviously, "flesh colored" bandages come in only one tone intended to match the skin of white persons, more or less. Why don't they come in boxes with varying shades and tones of flesh color? In the United States, being white has always conveyed certain advantages and preferences. But I can't find scriptural or theological grounds to support viewing my race as somehow superior to that of others, despite the fact that both the Bible and theology have been used, historically, to privilege white people. It reminds me of the gospel story of the rich man and Lazarus: In the afterlife, the rich man discovered he had not loved his neighbor as himself. The reality of white privilege does not mean that white people are somehow better or worse people by virtue of these systemic advantages. But having advantages based solely upon one's skin color does not represent the reign of God on earth; instead, it shows us a world of human construction in need of the healing, transforming power of Jesus Christ.

Many people today contend that because all are equal under the laws of the land, racial discrimination and injustices are a thing of the past. It's an argument suggesting that everyone has equal access to resources or the same opportunities to succeed. Yet, even today, when discrimination based upon skin color is illegal, there are still many indicators that the so-called playing field has not been leveled. Government statistics readily available online demonstrate that people of color are typically the last hired and the first laid off, which is especially evident in difficult economic times.[4] The unemployment rate for African Americans, Native Americans, and Hispanic Americans routinely exceeds the rate for white Americans and is often double that of the white population. Statistics show that people of color typically face higher conviction rates and longer sentences than white people who commit equivalent crimes. The percentages of African Americans, Native Americans, and other persons of color who live below the poverty line exceed poverty levels for white Americans—for reasons far more complex than the often cited and ill-informed claim that persons of color are less willing to work than their white counterparts. It's easy for us to attribute such disparities to individual behavior, whether lack of initiative or personal choices, but the source of such disparities is more complex. Many good people find the road to the American dream is laden with roadblocks and limited visibility.

Some decades ago, Christians began to understand the reality of both individual and what we call "systemic" sin. Not only do individuals act in ways that are contrary to God's will, but human institutions—even the church, at times—are often liable for systems, processes, and policies that do not glorify God or further human life and well-being. The Central Jurisdiction of the Methodist Church, which existed between 1939 and 1968, was a sinful human institution or structure, which supported a "separate but equal" status for African Americans reminiscent of the Jim Crow south. Whether we are aware of it or not, we all participate at least indirectly in systemic sin. For example, if we buy a pair of sandals at our local supercenter, we don't know the details of how it was made. Perhaps child labor was utilized in a foreign land. Thus, through our purchase, we actually perpetuate the system that harms those children who are forced to make sandals for pitiful wages to keep the retail prices low for the consumer. When we participate in various institutions and organizations, we should always keep our eyes open to practices that do not reflect the way of God in the world and then work to challenge and change them. In the gospels, Jesus constantly challenges the religious and political systems that claim to do God's will but allow some to prosper at the expense of others. Think of the woman caught in adultery in John 8. Although her behavior may, indeed, have been inappropriate, the system that would stone her and leave unpunished the man who was her accomplice is also sinful. Was her accomplice among those men preparing to cast the stones? Ignoring systemic sin or pleading ignorance doesn't make us less culpable. We must respond to the grace of God that leads us toward becoming the community that Jesus Christ calls us to be by the power of the Holy Spirit.

Babel and Pentecost

I remember a sermon by the theologian and historian, Justo González, which reinterpreted the stories of Babel (Genesis 11) and of Pentecost (Acts 2) so as to suggest that both stories are about unity and diversity. Often we read these stories together, claiming that Pentecost restores the unity lost through human arrogance, which was the central issue with the people's desire to build the tower of Babel. But what if the stories—like life itself—are nuanced, complex renderings of the commonalities and differences that God has created and wishes us to honor?

In Genesis 11, we are told that "the earth had one language" (verse 1), and this common language enabled the people to work together. But as with any gift from God, we can use language to honor God and one another or to undermine that goodness. The people created bricks and mortar and decided to build a city, with "a tower with its top in the heavens" so they could "make a name" for themselves (v. 4). Apparently, the people began to think highly of themselves and their power and ability, forgetting the limits of their humanity. They wanted to lift themselves up to God's level. The people thought they could construct a world where they would be God-like. Of course, we should not make the mistake of thinking this ancient society was egalitarian, that everyone held the same status or importance in the society. Those who were making the decisions are not likely the same as those who were making the bricks and sweating under the noonday sun. The story of the tower of Babel suggests that the powerful people wanted more power, not only over the people, but over God as well.

We deceive ourselves if we think that the common language had allowed for a true unity among the people. In many ways, the story reflects the development of human societies. The more advanced we become, the more stratified we become as some have great power and others do not. When God confused the people's language (v. 7), they scattered and left the building project unfinished. Only then did the disunity become readily apparent. While Genesis 11 is an etiological tale, intended to explain why there are different languages, God's decision to confuse the languages can be seen as a result of disunity among the people, rather than an overly ambitious unity. The people were not in right relationship with one another or with God. The various languages became a visible symbol of the divisions created by the human creature.

Acts 2 thus presents us with a story not simply of restored unity, but rather, of the unity in diversity that God creates and sustains. The text tells us that "when the day of Pentecost had come, they were all together in one place" (v. 1). In contrast to the restless migration of Genesis 11:2, the people of God waited in Jerusalem for the "promise of the Father" as they had been commanded by Jesus (Acts 1:4). They centered themselves in God through prayer (1:14), and the faithful who gathered there included the disciples, the women who had followed Jesus, and Jesus' brothers. Significantly, when the disciples decided to replace Judas with another man, they chose between two who had accompanied them throughout the whole of Jesus' ministry (1:21-22).[5] The story of Pentecost thus begins with the suggestion that before the coming of the Holy Spirit, the followers of Jesus were seeking to live in right relationship with God and one another. It would have been easy to fill those days of waiting with infighting, struggling for control of the movement. After all, when Jesus was with them, James and John once created a stir among the disciples over the question of who would be the greatest disciple (Mark 10:35-45). Given the society in which they lived, the men could easily have sent away the women, claiming it wasn't their place to be in that upper room. But it seems that some of Jesus' teachings actually did rub off on them because they were more concerned to include than to exclude. Even their choice of Matthias to complete the twelve leaders of the movement was not a matter of campaigning or debating, but of seeking God's will. And lest we should overlook this simple fact, there is also no mention of any physical characteristics beyond Matthias' gender, such that we don't know if his skin was light or dark, his hair was rough or smooth, as could have been the case in Palestine. It didn't matter what the chosen disciple looked like; only God's will mattered.

Then, the text tells us, a sound like a violent wind filled the house where all the people were waiting together in prayer. All of them were filled with the Holy Spirit—not just the twelve, but all of them—and they "began to speak in other languages, as the Spirit gave them ability" (2:4). The gift of the Holy Spirit didn't restore one common language; rather, it gave them the ability to speak and understand other languages than their own. The Holy Spirit didn't make everyone the same, but affirmed the differences that existed in Jerusalem by enabling Jesus' followers to adapt to those differences. Of course, the diverse people in Jerusalem responded in two ways upon hearing this cacophony of languages out of the mouths of simple Galileans: they either saw the remarkable power of God to bring unity in diversity, or they rejected the power of God as some drunken party trick. God created the gift of language in the first place, created the different languages at Babel, and then in the story of Pentecost, God reaffirmed the goodness of the various languages. Indeed, it would almost suggest that every Christian who is seeking the power of the Holy Spirit for the sake of God's reign on earth should learn more than one language! We should all learn to sing new songs.

Are we, today, more like the people in the story of the tower of Babel than like those in the story of Pentecost? Are we more inclined to build great cities and towers that stretch to the heavens to demonstrate our human power, or are we more inclined to share everything for the common good (Acts 2:43-46)? Those who sought to make a name for themselves became scattered and unable to speak to one another. Those who sought the will of God and chose to be in relationship with others, did "many signs and wonders" (2:43), had "glad and generous hearts" (2:46), and "day by day . . .

added to their number those who were being saved" (2:46). We, too, have the choice of accepting God's gift of the Holy Spirit and seeking to live in right relationship with all—not by imposing sameness, but by accepting the paradoxical unity found when we value and embrace the differences that God has created. There are no "outsiders" in God's reign, except for those who reject God's invitation to come to the table where all people sit side-by-side and share in the feast, even dipping bread in a common bowl.

If we take these biblical texts seriously, they suggest that white Americans are called by God to adapt to differences or to learn to appreciate them, rather than trying to make everyone speak English and adhere to white cultural norms. The world and its powers may try to enforce sameness, but God's Holy Spirit affirms the distinct languages and cultures that exist, and it calls us to affirm them. If the United States were to become a symbol of God's reign on earth, it wouldn't be because it becomes a totally white, English-speaking nation, but because it embraces, affirms and welcomes vastly different people, not into a "melting pot" but into a beautiful quilt that retains the varied colors and patterns woven by the hand of the living God. If the church is to be the body of Christ on earth, then the varieties of languages and cultural patterns will flourish by the power of the Holy Spirit. That is the Pentecost church. If The United Methodist Church in the United States is 90 percent white, can the power of the Holy Spirit be fully present among us? Can we be the church of Pentecost if we all look, speak, and act the same? Is the church in the United States willing to see and accept the gifts and spiritual wealth that are present in our global brothers and sisters, even if they don't share all of our cultural standards?

The true story told in the book, *Same Kind of Different as Me*, offers a glimpse of this Pentecost Spirit.[6] Ron, a wealthy white man, and Denver, a homeless African American man, meet after Ron's wife convinces him to help serve food to the homeless at the Union Gospel Mission. She tells Ron that he is to become friends with Denver, whom she'd seen in a dream and recognizes at the Mission. Ron figures that he'll take Denver to eat a few times and maybe help him get his life together. But as it turns out, Denver teaches Ron more about faith and friendship than he ever imagined possible. Ron, the well-to-do white man, is surprised to discover how much he can learn from Denver. God's grace breaks open his stereotypes and preconceived notions. In many ways, Denver's friendship enables Ron to survive the devastating death of his wife. Ron also becomes aware of the story behind Denver's homelessness, learning how the history of racism in the United States contributed to Denver's choice to live on the streets. It was a better option than to live in servitude to "the man," the white sharecropper who made sure his workers had no education, no support other than what he provided, and no opportunities for the future. *Same Kind of Different as Me* attests to the reality of unity in diversity when centered in God and open to being shaped by the Holy Spirit. It also demonstrates the very real brokenness that continues to exist in our society and world.

New Eyes to See Our Brokenness

Brokenness, the absence of right relationship, can only be healed by the power of God and the gifts of repentance and forgiveness. Repentance means turning back to God, making God the center of our lives again or for the first time. As I write these words, I am reminded that the 2012 General Conference held an Act of Repentance service in remembrance of our death-dealing history toward our Native American brothers and sisters. It is a history that most white Americans don't know and don't really care to know. Most white Americans haven't met any American Indians—largely because the government forcibly removed them from most of the continental United States over a century ago. Many white Americans will argue that they never harmed any Native persons. Why repent? Because the church was and continues to be complicit in the absence of right relationship to God and the Native American peoples. Not only did the church once participate in actions such as creating and sustaining Indian boarding schools designed to "civilize" Native Americans (once stated as, "kill the Indian and save the man"), the church continues to dehumanize in subtle ways. Repentance is more than apologizing. It's about living in radical relationship to others that society may marginalize, ignore, or even demonize. Such relationship is exemplified by Jesus Christ throughout the gospels and in the writings of Paul, and yes, both Jesus and Paul were criticized by society and sometimes even

Christian believers for including everyone in the church and at the table. Right relationship is at the heart of the Great Commandment to love God and to love our neighbor as ourselves.

I once heard a district superintendent tell his pastors that the Native American Comprehensive Plan had sent a letter to the Annual Conferences reminding them that the Book of Discipline of The United Methodist Church requires each church to have at least one person "to represent the need for better awareness of Native American contributions in the local church" (2008, para. 654). The superintendent went on to say, "I know this won't play well in your churches. So just let someone related to outreach ministries be designated." Rather than using the request as a teaching moment about the death-dealing ways of the world and even the institutional church, as well as the possibility for being Christ's agents of life abundant, he instead reinforced systemic sin. I know he later regretted the way he had presented it. But that is the power of systemic sin, which often pushes against transformation and leads us to act in ways we later regret. By contrast, repentance can be a powerful act of grace leading us to live into radical relationships, empowered by the love of the Holy Spirit.

Repentance is an acknowledgment that our human wisdom and power cannot lead us to healing and wholeness; only God in Christ in the Holy Spirit can offer us the fullness of life. It's an acknowledgment that we can never grasp the depths of our human brokenness. Repentance is an acknowledgment that even small acts of lovelessness toward others are not the way of Christ. Repentance turns our lives over again and again to the healing power of Christ, as we admit that we see in a glass dimly. Only God can heal the brokenness of our world, our society, and our churches. Only God can create unity in the midst of diversity, but we human beings have the responsibility to respond to God's initiative. John Wesley was clear that our faith journey is all a matter of grace and more grace. Yet God always gives us the choice to respond to the offer of grace or not. We can live in brokenness if we choose to ignore God's grace. But God will continue to seek the well being of the whole of creation. God offers salvation to all.

Salvation, which at its root means "wholeness" or "healing," is about becoming fully human as God created us to be. Our journey is not to become God; the tower of Babel clearly tells us that. Our journey is not to become Jesus Christ; there is and can be only one Jesus the Messiah who brings healing and wholeness. We are created by God to be fully human, and each of us is called to be a unique, irreplaceable person. We are created in the image of God and with vastly different gifts and abilities. As Paul writes in 1 Corinthians 12, there is one Spirit, but varieties of gifts, services, and activities. "To each is given the manifestation of the Spirit for the common good" (12:7). Differences are given by God to be used for the common good. But what happens when some are denied the ability to use their God-given gifts? What happens when some are closed off from opportunities to become fully who God created them to be? Brokenness. Most importantly, the body of Christ is incomplete; it yearns for the fullness of the Spirit's gifts present among the believers on behalf of the world.

Here we must contrast the power of the Holy Spirit as seen in Acts 2 with the desire for worldly power, as we saw in Genesis 11. Worldly power, especially in the absence of any awareness of the power of God, tends toward selfishness and the need to protect that power by any means. It is not unlike the powerful man Saul who persecuted the church and was closed off to how God might wish to change him. It took a life-altering experience on the road to Damascus for Saul to become Paul, the man willing to give up his power and position in society for the sake of the gospel of Christ in the world. Worldly power enslaved Africans, created Jim Crow laws, believed we could "kill the Indian and save the man," and now builds walls to define who is in and out along our borders, even though the land may have originally belonged to those whom we now claim to be "outsiders." Worldly power likes to exclude and to determine superiority and inferiority.

New Eyes to See God's Love

By contrast, the power of the Holy Spirit is the power of agape love; the bold, life-giving, relentless love of God who seeks to heal us, to make us whole, even when we choose the world's ways over God's will. Agape love is not the kind of love that permeates our society. God is love itself in the purest form: "Love is patient; love is kind; love is not envious or arrogant or boastful or rude. It does not insist on its own way; it is not irritable or resentful; it does not rejoice in wrongdoing, but rejoices in the truth" (1 Cor. 13:4-6). Saint Augustine described the Holy Spirit as the bond of love between God and the faithful, as well as among believers. The spirit of the world neither knows nor accepts this kind of life-giving, other-regarding, generous love. The church speaks often of love, but what if love requires us to be in radical relationship to the immigrant who speaks Vietnamese or Spanish or Tamil? What if love requires us to rethink our worship service in ways that incorporate other cultures? In his sermon, "Catholic Spirit," John Wesley proposed that the language we speak or the way we worship may differ, as long as the love of God and neighbor remains at the center of our faith in Jesus Christ. Do we love enough not only to welcome those who are different, but also to welcome the ways in which their very presence will transform our thinking, praying, and living?

When I was the pastor of a small Spanish-speaking church in Texas, one of our most faithful and love-filled members was a young man from Mexico. He seldom missed worship, always tithed what he earned, and volunteered to help with any work that needed to be done around the church. He had not been given the opportunity to finish high school in Mexico, but his intelligence and thirst for knowledge of God were evident. He had a passion for the gospel and an ability to share God's word with others. Sometimes, at the Sunday night Bible study, he would offer the lesson for us. One night, he opened the Bible to the book of Ruth and began to explain that the story of Naomi and Ruth is the story of immigrants. Like so many in Mexico who are unable to provide for themselves and their families, Naomi and Ruth left the land of Moab, having heard there was food in the land of Judah. He explained how he related to Naomi's desperation and willingness to make a long journey through the desert in the hope of surviving. I had never before seen the story of Ruth in light of the current immigration debates in the United States. I began to see with new eyes not only the story of Ruth, but also the reality of so many in the world who, because of human institutions and worldly powers, are unable to become who God has created them to be. When we meet our neighbor face-to-face as a brother or sister in Christ, the encounter has the potential to transform us in love and to deepen our love of God and neighbor.

As a white Christian, I am passionate about racial justice and helping The United Methodist Church to become a more visible representation of the reign of God on earth. I do not believe we are there, when the church in the United States is 90 percent white.[7] Many new church starts are in predominantly white neighborhoods, perhaps because we view them as economically viable compared to poorer neighborhoods where first generation immigrants reside. The gospel doesn't call us to go to the rich where our churches will be financially viable, but to go to all the world. I know of Cabinets in Annual Conferences who agonize over appointments to white congregations, but are willing to send almost anyone to serve as the pastor of a racial or ethnic congregation, especially if he or she is the "right color." Such actions reflect white privilege unconsciously at work. When I moved to Oklahoma and chose to become a member of an African American congregation, it baffled many people. One white United Methodist, upon asking where I worshiped, blurted out, "There aren't many white people at that church, are there?" I responded, "No, but the Holy Spirit is there."

Despite our many failures to recognize what it means to be white in the United States, I know that those who love God and neighbor can learn to see, understand, and dismantle white privilege. We can learn to speak other languages and to embrace other cultures without demeaning or rejecting our own. We can learn to sing a new song. Once when I gave a talk on white privilege, a pastor of many years was in attendance. He had never before heard of white privilege. The scales fell from his eyes that day, as he began to understand his whiteness and the advantages it carries. He began to search the internet to learn more about the reality of race and racism in the United States. He shared with others the PBS series, "Race: The Power of an Illusion," which explains how African Americans for many generations were unable to accumulate wealth in this country because they could not own property. Even as late as the 1940s, African Americans were excluded from government programs designed to facilitate home ownership. Anyone who understands the way wealth grows and is passed from generation to generation, even modestly, can grasp how centuries of exclusion could disadvantage people. This pastor read about the Tulsa Race Riots of the early twentieth century. Though commonly thought to have been caused by African Americans, he discovered that the riots were instigated by white Americans who feared the growing economic power of Tulsa's "Black Wall Street" and thus destroyed the homes and businesses of the African American community. This follower of Jesus began to wonder about the impact that media images of American Indians were having on his young grandson and decided to teach him to respect the culture and significance of Native peoples. I have witnessed the scales fall from eyes and seen transformation occur. God's grace will touch hearts and minds if we open ourselves to the real power of love.

There are many opportunities for white Christians to grow in their love of God and neighbor in relationship to racial and ethnic communities. Too often we wait for a mission trip to give us an opening where we can spend time experiencing different cultures. Or we visit a racial or ethnic congregation once, almost as if viewing a performance and conclude: "Wasn't that interesting! It made me uncomfortable, but it certainly was an interesting way to worship." Of course, white Christians can always slip back into a very white world and never worry about their brother or sister who is of a different race. That's the power of white privilege, at least for a few more decades when the country's demographics shift, bringing an end to the white majority.

People of color in the United States have always lived with a "double consciousness," to use the phrase of W.E.B. Du Bois. They live according to the expectations and viewpoint of the white majority culture and, at the same time, they live according to the cultural realities of their own communities. We might say, people of color in the United States have always lived in two worlds. They've had to negotiate white culture to survive. But white Americans can live within the boundaries of the white culture and never really encounter other ways of living. At least for a couple more decades, white Americans can live their whole lives without ever being in a setting where they are the minority amid a different culture.

Participating in Beloved Community

To understand white privilege and different cultures, we need to be intentional about participating in communities of color where we will not hold the position of privilege, power, or authority. It's perhaps a way of humbling ourselves when we could simply cling to our power and privilege. I was once part of a conversation between representatives of The United Methodist Church and the Catholic Church in the United States. During a discussion about a missional center that serves the Latino/a community, one person asked if The United Methodist Church and the Catholic Church could work together at the grassroots level despite our theological differences. The United Methodist episcopal representative, thinking the question was about reaching the Hispanic community, responded, "We've tried to get those people into our churches but they won't come." Turning to the Catholic episcopal representative, he said, "You have the same problem, don't you? They don't want to come to our churches." His statement was confirmed by a nod of the head and a smile. These leaders spoke in "us versus them" terms, essentially saying that the white churches were happy to allow Latinos to attend their congregations or parishes, but the Latinos didn't seem interested. To many of us who heard this exchange, it seemed that these church leaders viewed the world as white and believed the "right way" to live is according to white cultural standards. It's one thing to say anybody can come to our church; it's another thing to say that we will go to meet others on unfamiliar territory. I wonder where Jesus would go.

I began this process of intentionally participating in communities of color by joining a bilingual congregation in Texas sometime in 2003. My motives weren't very pure: I wanted to learn Spanish and thought worshiping there would help me to do so. But, of course, God had the last laugh because I soon was swept up in the Spirit's presence in that church. Eventually, I agreed to lead a Disciple Bible Study in Spanish, *Discipulado*, and was the only gringa in the class. My Spanish wasn't very good, but they were patient with me. I remember at the end of the many months of studying together, one of the church members told me that he was suspicious when I first joined the church. What was I doing there? Why wasn't I downtown at the big Anglo church? He said he waited for me to leave, but I kept coming back week after week. Only through my continual presence as a part of that community did he come to believe that my motives might be pure. Only by my willingness to be genuinely in community could he truly call me, hermana, sister. It was a matter of trust. The members of this church remain my beloved brothers and sisters in Christ, and I carry them in my heart, soul and mind, even though I no longer live in that city.

After my three years worshiping at the bilingual congregation, the district superintendent asked if I would be willing to serve as the part-time pastor of another small, Spanish-speaking congregation. I sincerely doubted that I could serve them well, since I had only begun to learn about the Latino/a culture and my own white privilege. I also knew that I would struggle to preach each Sunday in Spanish. Yet, by the grace of God I felt called to serve this community. I told them I would do my best to offer spiritual leadership and to help them become financially stable, but they would have to help me learn Spanish. We would have to teach one another. Sometimes in a sermon I would stop and ask, "Is this the right word?" Sometimes after church, the members would be giggling over something I'd said. Once, I talked about the "ears of God" in a sermon, but I used the Spanish word orejas—animal ears or ear flaps—rather than oidos, which are human ears and the sense of hearing. To Spanish speakers, it sounded funny. But I laughed and prayed and worshiped along with them, and my Spanish improved. Over time, I also began to find ways to use my white privilege on behalf of that congregation, drawing on my connections and my status in the church and community to strengthen the church's facilities and financial position. Looking back on those two years, I'm not sure how much they learned from me as their pastor, but there's hardly a day when I don't think about something I learned in that community of Christ-followers. There is a banner that hangs in my office, a going away gift from some members of the church, that reads, "Voy a hacer algo nuevo!" See I am doing a new thing! (Isa. 43:19). God continues to do a new thing within me and within our world.

When I relocated to Oklahoma, I visited many United Methodist congregations before choosing one where I felt the power of the Holy Spirit, the power of love, unmistakably present in my visits. It's a predominantly African American congregation. I am not the only white member of the church, but we are surely less than 10 percent of the congregation. Whether in worship, a Bible study, or some other church program, I grow and learn from spending time in a different cultural context and from placing myself in the "minority." Maybe I learn, in part, how to be nothing more than a child of God. But now, when I lead a Bible study or facilitate a group, I first acknowledge that I'm white and if I say something, well, too white, I encourage others to challenge me. I pray that I will never cease to learn about the real differences among human beings and to seek out the gifts that each person brings to the body of Christ. To see and to affirm the diversity of God's people who were created in the one, same image of God is to honor the Creator and Sustainer of all.

It has been almost ten years since I've worshiped regularly in an Anglo congregation. I haven't forgotten how to love, respect, and honor my white brothers and sisters. I am, after all, a white Christian in this society. But God has placed me on this journey for a reason: that I might speak the truth about racial injustice, white privilege, and the redeeming, reconciling, remarkable grace of God who created such a phenomenally diverse, yet biologically similar human race. The truth is we are all one human race called to be in right relationship with God, one another, ourselves, and even the whole of creation. To be sure, the new creation will not be a place of sameness but a radically relational reality where each of us can be fully who God has created us to be. A place where love will be the center of our lives, our hearts, our communities, our world. A place where love will be all in all.

Some might ask why I should care so passionately about racial justice. After all, my ancestors never enslaved anyone; they did not uproot any Native Americans; they did not fight at the Alamo or intern Japanese Americans in World War II. My relatives did not even live in the southern United States during the time of legal seg-regation. Why should I care so deeply about racial justice, when it means that I will likely have to give up some worldly power and privilege in exchange for a more just society? The answer is simple. It is the way of Jesus Christ. I am called by God and empowered by the Holy Spirit to help dismantle institutions that serve to deny persons the opportunity to become fully human as God created them to be. I am called by God and empowered by the Holy Spirit to learn how to love my neighbor as myself and to share this knowledge with others. God is not done with me yet. God is not finished with the church yet. And God is certainly not yet finished with this world. The Holy Spirit, the bond of love, is at work drawing us together as one people, one body strengthened by the giftedness and cultures of its different members. It is this vision and future which continues to draw me, inspire me, and give me hope. It is the new creation that one day will be our home.

This is my song to a new dawn.

Notes

1. For a scientific analysis, see Alan R. Templeton, "Human Races: A Genetic and Evolutionary Perspective, "*American Anthropologist*, New Series, Vol. 100, No. 3 (Sept. 1998), pp. 632-650.

2. See, for example, Steve Garner, *Whiteness: An Introduction* (New York: Routledge, 2007) or Beth Frankel Merenstein, *Immigrants and Modern Racism* (Boulder, CO: Lynne Rienner Publishers, 2008).

3. Peggy McIntosh, "Unpacking the Invisible Knapsack," in *White Privilege: Essential Readings on the Other Side of Racism*, 3rd ed., ed. Paula S. Rothenberg (New York: Worth Publishers, 2008). The essay is widely available online.

4. Government statistics can be found at www.fedstats.gov or at the federal department websites.

5. Clearly, the system was far from perfect, given that women were excluded from the decision based upon social norms that afforded women no legal rights or status in society.

6. Ron Hall and Denver Moore, *Same Kind of Different as Me* (Nashville: Thomas Nelson, 2006).

7. See the statistical report "Lay Membership—Racial/Ethnic/Gender (2004–2009)" at http://www.gcfa.org/data-services.

For Further Reading

Hall, Ron and Denver Moore. *Same Kind of Different as Me*. Nashville: Thomas Nelson, 2006.

McIntosh, Peggy. "White Privilege: Unpacking the Invisible Knapsack," in *White Privilege*, edited by Paula S. Rothenberg. New York: Worth Publishers, 2008. [McIntosh's essay is widely available online.]

Robinson, Elaine. *Race and Theology*. Nashville: Abingdon Press, 2012.

CHAPTER SIX

Becoming a Beloved Community: An African American Perspective

Rosetta E. Ross

Introduction

As a child of the U.S. Civil Rights Movement, I grew up and entered adulthood with hope for what race relations in the United States and the world could become. The source of my hope was wide-ranging work to dismantle policies and practices (and even imaginary concepts) that divided humanity into assorted groups of haves and have-nots. The Civil Rights era was a time of great change and substantial momentum around a variety of "social justice" issues (even though some issues had to emerge after the burst of the mid-century Civil Rights heyday). Movement workers wanted to ensure that persons across the social and economic spectrum of society participated in and benefited from public life. Their goals were bold. They wanted to reorder social policies and practices to give people across all economic and educational levels access to mechanisms that arranged society, and to enhance the material situation of the country's poor people, who, in the middle of the twentieth century still were overwhelmingly people of color. Seized by the belief that it was possible to develop a society that affirms everyone, many Civil Rights advocates sought to realize a broad vision of equality that they called "beloved community." Momentum of that era was so strong that persons frequently collaborated across lines of party, class, race, social station, and ideological persuasion to overcome the nation's deep and tragic legacy of racial discrimination.

Still, not everyone who lived through that time in the United States remembers it as hopeful. For many, the era signaled a particularly destructive challenge to reigning social conventions. Others recall the violence that accompanied almost every advancement against suppressive racial norms. There are many perspectives on the mid-twentieth century U.S. Civil Rights Era. Today, and for about the past three decades we have been living in a time when there is a parity (and sometimes a majority) of cultural actors and voices as fully bent on eroding and reversing hard-won Civil Rights victories as workers of the Civil Rights era were bent on winning them. These voices challenge and undermine the value of some generalized ideals that knit persons together into one nation across differences of race and ethnicity, class, gender, sexuality, education level, age, and so on.

Civil Rights leaders counted on the significance of those generalized ideals that helped knit society together. At that time, in spite of many inequalities, across much of the culture, there was a sense of decency that helped define for many people the meaning of being a person and of being a member of society. That sense of decency served as a basis upon which challenges were mounted against exclusionary practices and through which good will was gathered to propel the Civil Rights Movement forward. Even during the most severe times of discrimination and racial animosity, these generalized ideals—such as respecting the human dignity of all persons; lending a helping hand; sharing one's benefits, knowledge, and influence to care for neighbors; practicing social responsibility as an expression of citizenship and connection to others—formed a foundation upon which conversations and negotiations about race could occur. Today, such norms may even be labeled as anti-democratic sentiments that call for a neglect of personal responsibility in order to redistribute wealth through the structures of government.

My identity was formed and informed by a community of persons who identified themselves as practicing Christians. Because of their understanding of what it meant to be a person and to be a Christian, it seemed natural to me that the Civil Rights Movement integrated values of egalitarianism and interdependence as a basis for its claims. The expectation that persons would respect and care for others resonated with the Christianity I knew, and that I hoped could help substantially change society. This hope persisted in me in spite of the period of my childhood and youth when deep traditions of segregation and discrimination were practiced all around me. And even though we currently live in an era that often dismisses broad social egalitarianism as irrelevant, when I look back through the history of my family and my race in the United States, this hope persists. Perhaps it does so especially because I still see in the ideals and collaboration of many persons across diverse religious traditions a similar desire to be knit together as a community of inhabitants of this society and of the planet, in spite of our differences.

My African American Background

In the genealogy of my family, five generations ago, my paternal great, great grandfather Pink Ross helped found St. Daniel Methodist Episcopal Church near the rural village of Dorchester, South Carolina. Pink Ross had been enslaved. That he overcame enslavement by acquiring more than 100 acres of land and helping to found a post-Emancipation church for formerly enslaved persons is a source of generational family pride. Pink's great grandson, my father, settled with my mother near Morris Chapel Methodist Episcopal Church, the congregation in Dorchester that my mother, her parents, and her grandparents attended. My siblings and I grew up as fourth generation members of the Morris Chapel congregation.

Dorchester is situated in the region of South Carolina called the low country, because of its proximity to the Atlantic Ocean. The South Carolina low country was once known for agricultural eminence, especially in producing rice. Some enslaved Africans brought to the region were captured particularly for skill in rice production. During the mid-eighteenth through late-nineteenth centuries, South Carolina rice growers (and later cotton and tobacco growers) used free labor of enslaved persons to accumulate massive wealth, including resources used to finance southern efforts to maintain the status quo during the Civil War. Today, South Carolina's low country is known most for tourism, since that area of the state includes Charleston, Kiawah Island, Hilton Head, Pawley's Island, Daniel Island, Sullivan's Island, John's Island, and Myrtle Beach. Coastal South Carolina's colonial legacy of splendor through enslavement also is included among the state's tourist attractions.

Dorchester is about thirty miles inland from the central South Carolina coast. During my childhood, and even more so for the generations that preceded me, Dorchester and the surrounding region were farming territory. Against the natural beauty of the area's lush vegetation, fields of cotton, tobacco, and corn dominated landscape that was not residential or forest terrain. My family worshiped at Morris Chapel Church with neighbors who shared life together as worshipers and friends, and beyond church with neighbors who were Baptists and Pentecostals, as well as with neighbors who preferred not to participate with either of these two congregations. Many families in Dorchester grew produce and livestock for market on large and small scales. Almost all families planted vegetable gardens, and several also raised livestock for food. Because of South Carolina's temperate climate, gardening continued well into the winter. While most families cultivated vegetable gardens and raised livestock to feed themselves, members of the community always shared produce with one another. In spite of the community's segregation, by the mid-twentieth century, it was not unusual for this sharing to cross racial lines. Cross-racial hospitality in sharing farm produce, and other occasional reciprocities, did not overcome or seek to overcome the community's culture of segregation and discrimination. In fact, such cross-racial sharing may even have served to solidify racial politics by smoothing over the reality of race-based political and economic brutality.

Still, there was in the practice of sharing from one's produce intentional imparting of practices of decency and of manners that functioned, in spite of the double entendre, to convey what it was to be a person as a member of a community with other persons. There was among the community of African Americans who nurtured me a sense of vocation about what it meant to be a decent human being. This sense of vocation was communicated as one learned from others that she was valued as a person and as she was taught to so value others. There also was in my community the idea that all persons exist as members of society who were expected, with the assistance of relationships to others, to grow, develop, and improve themselves to become productive, contributing members of society and to include among their productivity contributing to and assisting in the growth and development of other persons. This vocation of being a person might be described as enjoying oneself among the members of the community. Significant gratification was derived from the ways one's contributions affirmed and supported others and enhanced general well-being of and in the community.

Passing on values such as conceptions of decency and practices of manners was the means by which African Americans in my community prepared children to be contributing social actors. While the meaning of the term decent today often is narrowed to exclude its less expansive reference to participating in and helping ensure a certain quality of life, the more expansive meaning of decency is what was communicated to me. To live a decent life included expressing certain human characteristics in relationship to other persons and to inhabit one's own life in a way that valued and respected other persons. My parents and other elders in the community frequently use the term "common decency" to identify what they expected of persons in relating to one another. "It's only common decency to share," they might say, for example, "if you have more than what you need." Having manners sometimes is associated with obsequiousness, but it was taught to me as an important element of showing respect for others and one's self. "Thank you," "please," "you're welcome," "you first," "may I help," and even "that's not right (fair)" were taught to me as elements of respecting and protecting the humanity of others.

During my childhood, in spite of efforts to smooth over overt practices of racism, the generalized perspective that African Americans were not worthy of being treated decently or of being respected through ordinary customs of manners was a person-to-person reflection of deeper political and economic subordination that was the order of the day. At that time, the view that black persons existed as instruments to enhance the lives of white persons was a pervasive idea about African Americans that dominated the cultural imagination. While there may have existed at some level a sense of sharing values across community and racial lines; like other villages, towns, and cities across the country, on issues of race, the community of my childhood was broken. Housing and institutional patterns reflected the antebellum and Reconstruction legacy of segregation and subordination. African Americans lived in less visible areas. Morris Chapel Methodist Church was a "black" congregation, and white Methodists in Dorchester attended First Church in the nearby town of Harleyville. When I moved into the larger world, it was not difficult to discern similarities of my experiences, on many levels, with what was occurring in the lives of African Americans elsewhere, including continuing and heightening challenges to various practices of racial subordination though momentum of the Civil Rights Movement. While not identical to practices of racism in rural areas, racial segregation and subordination in U.S. towns, cities, and suburban areas arose from the same ideas about the culturally contrived instrumental meaning of black existence.

I have wondered from time to time what accounted for formerly enslaved Black Christians maintaining ties with the Methodist Episcopal Church (MEC) immediately after Emancipation, especially given the denomination's mixed history on issues of race. I do not know the origin of my ancestors' interaction with Methodism—whether they initially chose the denomination or whether it was chosen for them. The wider history of African Americans and Protestant Christianity suggests the denomination may have been chosen, since one major reason Protestantism became the primary vehicle for religious expression among Africans in the United States was the enslavers' fears about the autonomous religious meetings of black persons. The planned 1739 Stono Rebellion in Charleston—likely organized by enslaved Congolese men and women who blended the colonial Catholicism they encountered in Africa with Congolese traditional religions—resulted in the South Carolina Negro Act of 1740, which forbade unsupervised African assemblies.[1] Similar policies were enacted in other areas of the South. When the 1740 Negro Act was developed, most Africans enslaved in the colonies did not practice Christianity. Around that time, however, Northern and Southern planters and primarily Protestant Christian missionaries (including those of the fledgling Methodist Episcopal Church, MEC) were deliberating the merits and potential challenge of evangelizing enslaved people. A major sticking point of their deliberations was how to engage the egalitarian implications of Christian baptism for the material relationship of enslavers and enslaved persons.

Although MEC General Conferences repeatedly debated the issue of enslavement, some Methodist evangelists in the South accepted the eighteenth-century theological logic that baptism did not denote social equality and that Christianization would make Africans better to be enslaved. This logic conquered planters' fears and gave Protestant missionaries access to populations of enslaved persons, an opportunity for which they had spent years negotiating. By the end of the eighteenth century, "mainline Protestantism" became the predominant form of religious expression among enslaved Africans. Nevertheless, debates about enslavement persisted within the MEC, and in 1845 this ongoing debate caused the MEC to split into the Northern and Southern denominational branches. After Emancipation, Pink Ross and others, for whatever reasons, continued to throw in their lots with the MEC. By the time of Reconstruction, when Pink helped build the first St. Daniel Church, the MEC had become familiar as a religious practice among Africans in the region. This occurred in spite of the reality of the 1845 denominational split into two entities affirming and opposing enslavement. That some black persons persisted in their affiliation with the MEC after Emancipation is interesting in view of this being a period when the African Methodist Episcopal (AME) Church actively evangelized across the South, causing many black Methodists to leave the segregation of the MEC for self-rule in the AME Church or the congregational polity of Baptists. The possibilities for education may have contributed to some black persons choosing to maintain ties with the MEC. In spite of and alongside its nineteenth-century racial challenges, one important legacy of the MEC is its contribution to education of black persons. White volunteers from the MEC and the MEC, South, participated with literate black persons and with members of other denominations in the American Missionary Association's work to educate African Americans after Emancipation. Development of instruction at the primary, secondary, and, eventually, college level precipitated development of public primary and secondary education for African Americans as well as establishment of a system of black colleges.

In the early twentieth century, millions of African Americans left the South en masse during the Great Migrations that resulted in the first large urban black populations in cities of the North, the Midwest, and the West. One of the most significant cultural practices black persons carried with them as they migrated North was their adapted forms of primarily Protestant Christianity. As they experienced different contexts of segregation in U.S. cities, various forms of Christianity helped urban black populations continue to construct conceptions about being persons and otherwise survive challenges they faced in starting and developing their communities. Along with blacks in the South, African Americans who affiliated with the MEC in U.S. cities encountered the denomination's checkered legacy of racial discrimination. By 1939, two decades of black urban dwellers had participated in the first wave of the Great Migration. During that year, the MEC overcame its North/South division by yielding to southern insistence that black members of the denomination formally be segregated into a separate entity, the Central Jurisdiction. In addition to formalizing racial segregation, this action, affecting black MEC members across the country, also (re)formalized almost thirty years of economic discrimination by denying African Americans significant access to the denomination's financial and institutional resources, even though black persons supported development of those resources through the practice of apportioned congregational and conference giving. As the Civil Rights Movement gathered momentum, formation of The United Methodist Church (UMC), through union of the Methodist Episcopal and Evangelical United Brethren denominations in 1968, prompted several years of work to abolish the Central Jurisdiction. However, the legacy of structural segregation and subordination persists as challenges in the lives of African Americans who encounter in the larger society and a variety of institutional contexts, such as The United Methodist Church, halting efforts to overcome the systemic racism, structural segregation, and economic subordination of the denomination's and the country's past. MEC/UMC members both supported and opposed developments of the Civil Rights Era. Similar to many other Civil Rights workers, MEC members who supported the Civil Rights Movement understood its ideals as prompted by Christian teachings and scripture.

Resources in Scripture for Considering Issues of Broken Community

Christian scripture provides ample examples of mutuality in community through stories, teachings, and themes that affirm universality and reconciliation. Sometimes these examples emerge in biblical texts about broken community. Other examples are presented as stories of persons living in community in ways that model values that scripture teaches. Scripture is the normative source of authority for belief among Christians. However, since at least the time of Constantine (272–337), there has steadily developed among Christians tensions about the relationship of belief to practice and practice to belief in determining the meaning of being Christian. Some persons argue that principles and examples within scripture have to do with spiritual, ideal relations between persons, and so do not have practical implications for social life. Belief is asserted as the essential element of Christian identity almost apart from and in spite of what persons do. The converse perspective, that a specific kind of practical behavior is essential to Christian identity and supersedes the importance of belief, is asserted by other Christians. This debate even is evident within scripture in James' assertion that "Faith without works is . . . dead" (2:26). Those who agree with this perspective contend that what persons do is more important as an indicator of the spiritual nature of Christian identity. While there is some appeal in both of these perspectives, looking through the history of African American interactions with Christian justification of practices of racial subjugation as consistent with belief about spiritual egalitarianism, I lean more toward practical implications of scriptural themes in my interpretations of the Bible.

I first read the book of Acts for my own curiosity and edification as a young adult. I was captivated by passages in Acts 4 and 5 describing the early Christian community's collaboration and sharing, especially the assertion that "[t]here was not a needy person among them," because the community developed a social witness demonstrating that "great grace was upon them all" (4:34, 33). In my youthful idealism, I welcomed this Acts passage because it suggested norms of egalitarianism, social responsibility, and compassion that coincided with values taught in my childhood and the Civil Rights Movement, and because it contradicted practices of racism, class cleavages, and sexism plaguing society. These ideals modeled in Acts continue to inform my understanding of what constitutes a good society, and remain for me an example from Christian scripture of what it means to strive to live together in what U.S. Civil Rights Movement participants called "beloved community." Many today might argue or object to implications of this passage as unrealistic for how we should live in society. However, what I continue to see in Acts 4 is intentional action taken by persons who made conscious decisions, without compulsion, to share in order to ensure the well-being of all members of the community.

While Acts 4 conveys communal norms of egalitarianism, social responsibility, and compassion, early verses in Acts 5 express an expectation that members of the community will engage one another honestly. Peter's challenge to Ananias (and Sapphira) is not that they should have given what they had and earned. Instead he challenges them to take responsibility for voluntarily bearing their identity as Christians and to engage members of the community honestly. We do not have the back story of how first-century Acts Christians acquired their resources. One primary source of "old" wealth in the United States accrued for persons who generation after generation after generation acquired resources through free labor as enslavers of Africans, and who, after the U.S. Civil War, especially in the South, continued for seven more generations to legislate or terrorize economic peonage through Jim Crow laws and violence. Today, there are debates about whether the economic legacy of chattel enslavement and the social legacy of racial peonage continue to operate or to have meaning for social and political life in the United States. In spite of many and deep changes that have occurred in U.S. society, there is reason to challenge the truth of arguments that assert that there are no longer legacies of enslavement or that there do not persist institutional and social structures that privilege descendants of Europeans.

Some Sources of Broken Community: Beliefs about Scarcity and Systemic Racism

Issues of racism, like other challenges of broken community, often have to do with economics, especially access to and control over resources, as well as with social or political power, two arenas that manage access to and control of resources. Dominant control of material resources in the United States required structuring policies as well as customs that regulated diverse and vast arenas of life. For example, taking charge of Native lands involved making the determination that the land could be taken, construction and dissemination of ideas denigrating the humanity of Native peoples, using lethal violence (including the military) to capture lands, removal of Native peoples from the lands, sometimes negotiating agreements (including federal treaties) with Native peoples about lands, violating negotiated agreements about lands through courts or the Congress, and an array of other policies and practices. In the case of African Americans, institutionalizing enslavement as a mechanism to provide free labor also involved development and regulation of diverse and vast policy and customary arenas. For instance, similar to development of discourses that denigrated Native Americans, enslavement required establishing the determination that Africans should be enslaved and constructing and disseminating ideas that disparaged Africans' humanity. Content of these discourses included negative assessments of Africans' intellectual capacity, moral propensities, hygienic practices, physical appearance, and so on. In addition to discursive policies and customs, enslavers also developed material mechanisms and structures to facilitate access to free labor. This included mechanisms to capture and transport Africans across large areas of the African continent, including collaborating with various African ethnic groups in the capture of others. It also included dishonest business practices, since the same Africans who captured and sold other Africans to European enslavers often were themselves later captured and enslaved. Shipping companies in various parts of Europe participated in transporting Africans across the Atlantic or north to Europe. The same shipping companies also transported raw and manufactured goods that resulted from practices of enslavement. In what was becoming the United States, northern and southern colonies collaborated similarly in exchange of enslaved persons, raw materials, and manufactured goods. The absence of labor costs due to enslavement meant that at a variety of levels it was extremely lucrative to participate in controlling and trading products derived from free labor. There were other areas where policies and practices developed as theologians, politicians, and educators constructed rhetorical support for economic ventures related to this free labor. Structuring this interrelated web of arrangements occurred over time, but ultimately worked together to facilitate development of economic control. Recognition of the reality of this systematization accounts for the regular assertion by anti-racism leaders that the difference between racism and prejudice is the systematic nature of racist practices. While practices within the system of racism differ in relationship to various racialized groups, they all on some level emerged in relationship to economics and issues of access and control.

As a set of practices that is systematized, racism so pervades culture as to easily engender racist practices by people of color against one another. In addition to experiencing racial discrimination firsthand, growing up African American in the United States during the mid- to late-twentieth century often meant falling into the binary trap of viewing issues of race as exclusively related to blackness and whiteness. For example, even though I participated in and knew that school integration in Dorchester County included dismantling the separate school district that existed for Native children as well as the separate systems for black and white children, I was a young adult before I considered that most discussions of race were oblivious to the history of Native peoples in North America, and especially the control of the natural resources that provided for and structured Native Americans' lives. It was much later in my life that I began trying to contemplate the meaning of my birth, growth, and development on land that belonged by "law" to my parents, but that never was ethically transferred out of the hands of Native peoples. Racism practiced against Native Americans was not the same as that practiced against African Americans; however, in both cases, the source of racial practices in the United States related to the desire to garner and control material resources.

Viewing the earth's resources as scarce fuels many perspectives about conquest and control. While there are real limits of some natural resources, ideas that there exists a generalized scarcity of resources sufficient to care for the world's population never have been proven. Unfortunately, views about scarcity structure many social institutions and, thereby, often contribute to animosity between groups by creating an artificial scarcity. It is not surprising that conceptions of scarcity are deeply connected to determinations that persons from different racial and ethnic groups should be excluded or devalued. This view has played a substantial role in identifying some human beings with the natural world and in need of being conquered alongside it. Social and political structures that separated, ranked, and broke apart humanity in a variety of ways resulted from views about scarcity and difference. Sometimes the philosophical perspective that human beings naturally are at war with one another compounded the tendency to seize control over resources and justified development of structures that negated the humanity of some persons in order to protect the dominance of others. Surprisingly, at the same time that racial structures of separation and domination were being developed, concepts about the innate rights of human beings also were emerging. The establishment of myths and stereotypes depicting some persons as not human or not fully human attempted to conceal these developing ideas about human rights and to strengthen the systemic racism that supported economic control. The view that what is needed is scarce and the practice of concealing and qualifying implications of social norms have had long-term effects on our cultural imagination, making it difficult to envision ways to construct a society that values, or even believes as possible, the development of a nurturing, welcoming, and egalitarian human community.

Continuing Impediments: Two Challenges to Movement toward Beloved Community

Perhaps the two greatest impediments to movement toward beloved community are disbelief that systemic racism exists and inertia of the human will. Many persons do not believe that systemic racism exists.[2] While reasons for disbelief vary, perhaps most common is the view that systemic racism is too farfetched and too much like science fiction to be real. So often the concept systemic racism evokes an image of a sinister gathering to craft of a network of ideas and practices all at once in order to subordinate persons based on race. The concept also often is conceived as arising from the minds of persons so malevolent that they could not be real. While the term "systemic racism" does identify an interrelated network of ideas and practices that have had deadly consequences, the emergence of the system arose from ordinary business processes undertaken by respectable, though ambitious, persons seeking to achieve certain economic goals. The development of systems of racism emerged in accord with other processes of human history. Some persons sought avenues and alliances to accomplish economic goals and in the process structured moral norms, political policies, and economic processes to facilitate accomplishment of their goals. For example, in the early colonial era, because most Northern and Southern planters forbade evangelization of enslaved persons (which threatened to end access to free labor) Protestant evangelizers adjusted their messages, becoming allies with planters in achieving their economic goals, by affirming the benefit of Christian evangelization to enslavement.[3] This one example occurred, not as a backroom deal among hunched-back ogres, but evolved openly, over time in discourses in churches and homes, among leaders of society.

Another impediment to moving toward beloved community is the reluctance to change what may appear to be working. Unwillingness to critically examine or seek to address issues of racial discrimination sometimes relates substantially more to the comfort level persons have developed with the way things are than it does to persons' support of racism. It is not unusual that change requires (or appears to require) more time and attention than maintaining the status quo. Most persons prefer to continue living with the familiar, and sometimes become so deeply invested in the familiar that it is disruptive to entertain the idea of things being different. In some instances, persons will undertake violence to avoid speech as well as behavior aimed at change. Both investment in one's comfort level as well as investment in racial subordination are impediments that reflect inertia of the human will. Even persons who express intellectual commitment to racial justice and racial reconciliation find it difficult to achieve much alteration of attitudes and behaviors because there often is not significant thought given to the depth of challenge presented by systemic racism or to the level of commitment as well as the amount of time and energy necessary to overcome the ordinary inertia of persons whose lives never are discomfited by systemic racism.

Looking to a New Dawn: Some Reasons for Hope

Two historically consistent elements of the UMC's legacy are sources of hope for race relations in our future. First, while the UMC's history includes the denomination's inability to stay a direct, consistent course opposing racially subordinating policies and practices, there also is in United Methodist history the positive reality that, in general, there was acceptance of diverse perspectives on racial subordination. Most important in this regard is the fact that there almost always were consistent and clear voices of white allies and leaders who opposed various denominational policies instituting practices of racism. The UMC's heterogeneous legacy on issues of race is, on the one hand, a history to be overcome. On the other hand, that legacy is one element of the theological pluralism that once was a deeply held value of the denomination. Pluralism provided space for persons to try within a community of believers to live out their faith as members of the UMC, while sometimes deeply disagreeing about what it meant to do so. Today the current political climate that eschews collaboration and compromise, as well as current efforts in the larger society to tamp down dissent and difference are evident in the denomination's discussions at every level as some persons attempt to obliterate the United Methodist legacy of pluralism in order to make all Methodists speak with one voice. While pluralism sometimes makes decision-making processes very difficult, its presence also means having enough room for a variety of voices and should inevitably issue in a variety perspectives and ways of carrying out the denomination's ministry. In a nation and church as diverse as ours, recognition and embrace of plurality is necessary to interweave everyone into the fabric of our identity. Doing so is difficult, but to be intentionally diverse is the essence of what makes democracy work, and, more important to United Methodism, it encompasses the reality of being the diverse people of God. It is the meaning of being beloved community. Pluralism is a resource from our past that, if accepted and reintegrated, could help us overcome some of the long-term acrimony that threatens the vitality of who we are.[4] Embracing pluralism and our racial and ethnic diversity risks failing to achieve the ends we envision because we sometimes will be overtaken by those with different views, but embracing pluralism also promises to make United Methodists a community of believers who face as a reality the difficulty of seeking to be one body of many members.

That legacy of consistent voices opposing racial segregation and subordination is a second element of the denomination's history that serves as a source of hope. In spite of a history of the UMC wavering on racial issues, it is possible to see and important to take account of the consistent presence of perspectives and actions by persons within the denomination who vocally asserted that racial hierarchy is neither natural nor good. Many persons who collaborated across racial lines as allies to and leaders alongside African Americans to make the Civil Rights Movement a reality did so out of their sense of what it meant to be faithful believers. There is a legacy of cross-racial efforts to address the country's racial challenges in church and parachurch work of persons who also sought to actualize their understanding of what it meant to be Christian. They worked as clergy and lay leaders during the antebellum era; as educators during the Reconstruction era; as women's group members and leaders and as human relations agents around the turn of the century; and as members and allies of organizations such as the National Association for the Advancement of Colored People (NAACP) during the early to mid-twentieth century. They developed the understructure for mid-twentieth-century collaboration on race issues. Many of these persons included among their work, teaching ideals of racial reconciliation to the next generation, and they served as advisors to youth organizations that discussed the possibilities of enacting those ideals. These youth advisors made way for youth and young adult leaders in race relations as they intentionally developed the initial meetings and then collaborative experiences of young people they mentored.

Young people were especially, though not exclusively, important to the momentum that drove cross-racial civil rights work. By the time the mid-twentieth-century began to take shape, thousands of persons who were being nurtured in or who had entered youth and young adulthood having participated as leaders and members of Christian youth organizations carried within them ideas about and experiences of racial reconciliation. Adult leaders and advisors of youth groups and student Christian organizations had developed decades-long programs of education, conversation, and engagement that placed the legacy of race relations between black and white persons as centrally important to the development of future leaders for Christianity in the United States. When the Civil Rights Movement began to unfold, and sometimes as an element of the Movement's unfolding, these young people developed or took up a variety of practices that brought to life their theoretical and experimental encounters of practicing racial equality. Many of these youth were members of the mid-twentieth century Student Christian Movement, some nurtured in the Methodist Episcopal Church. The religious conviction that they were participating in work that manifested what Christianity ought to and could become gave an intensity to their actions.

Within United Methodism, there also emerged collaborations and alliances similar to those that developed in the larger society. The processes put in place to develop a United Methodism that sought to overcome its racial legacy included structural developments to address it. Black United Methodists initiated some of these developments through a series of meetings seeking to ensure continuation of their substantial participation as equal members of the newly formed United Methodist denomination. From these meetings developed two important denominational structures, the 1968 creation of the General Church Commission on Religion and Race and the emergence of the permanent para-structural unit Black Methodist for Church Renewal. In addition to these important structural developments, the momentum of redress in the larger society influenced other developments in the denomination, including opening of opportunities for African American participation within the denomination across a wide variety of representative and administrative roles.[5]

As I imagine him, my great, great Grandfather Pink Ross would look through history to affirm United Methodists for strides that have been made in the face of systemic racism; he also would, I imagine, admonish and encourage United Methodists to keep moving forward.

There still are challenges. There has been change. There is hope.

When there is hope, there still is work to be done.

Notes

1. The 1739 Stono Rebellion in Charleston, South Carolina—which precipitated the 1740 Act—was thought to have originated among Africans who gathered autonomously for religious observance. See Albert Raboteau, *"Slave Religion: The "Invisible Institution" in the Antebellum South,* (New York: Oxford, 1978), 116, and Peter Wood, *Black Majority: Negroes in Colonial South Carolina from 1670 through the Stono Rebellion,* (New York: Knoff, 1974), especially chapter 12.

2. United Methodist Bishop James Thomas notes the historic development of ideas and practices I am identifying here as "systemic racism." Thomas writes, "Unless one remembers that the making of the American mind began long before the founding of the nation, one will not understand the patterns and structures of racial segregation. In 1619, a Dutch ship brought twenty 'Negers' to the colonies and sold them to the planters to work in the tobacco fields. This established slavery in the colonies 170 years before the ratification of the Constitution in 1789. So powerful did the institution of slavery become, that it seemed to some an eternal institution." See James S. Thomas, *Methodism's Racial Dilemma: The Story of the Central Jurisdiction* (Nashville: Abingdon Press, 1992), 33.

3. Albert Raboteau, *Slave Religion: The "Invisible Institution" in the Antebellum South* (New York: Oxford, 1978). See chapter 3, "Catechesis and Conversion," especially 102–103, 108–109.

4. J. Philip Wogaman argues similarly in Methodism's Challenge in Race Relations, where he writes that conflict may bring about a creative encounter: "Effective strategy in The Methodist Church seems particularly weakened by a general inability to conceive of creative uses of conflict and controversy within the fellowship of the church. 'Harmony' and 'unity' have often been overemphasized to the exclusion of other important values which define the nature of the church, with the result that harmony and unity are themselves more apparent than real. In this situation there is a danger that strategic efforts to change the status quo of racial segregation will be interpreted as disruptions of the fellowship rather than as desirable creative innovation in harmony with the basic values of the church." See J. Philip Wogaman, *Methodism's Challenge in Race Relations: A Study of Strategy* (District of Columbia: Public Affairs Press, 1960), 70.

5. Thomas notes that some of the increase in opportunities to serve in representative roles occurred in response to creation of the Central Jurisdiction. See Thomas, *Methodism's Racial Dilemma*, 149.

For Further Reading

Thomas, James. *Methodism's Racial Dilemma: The Story of the Central Jurisdiction*. Nashville: Abingdon Press, 1992.

Shockley, Grant S., editor. *Heritage and Hope: The African American Presence in United Methodism*. Nashville: Abingdon Press, 1991.

Wogaman, J. Philip, *Methodism's Challenge in Race Relations: A Study of Strategy* (District of Columbia: Public Affairs Press, 1960), 70.

CHAPTER SEVEN

From God-Community to a Beloved Community

Samuel John Royappa

Biblical Understanding of Community

Danny Dutton, an eight-year-old boy from Chula Vista, California, explained God like this: "One of God's main jobs is making people. He makes them to replace the ones that die, so there will be enough people to take care of things on earth. He doesn't make grownups, just babies. I think because they are smaller and easier to make. That way he doesn't have to take up his valuable time teaching them to talk and walk. He can just leave that to mothers and fathers." What a profound and powerful way of understanding *community* as "people"! God created and continues to create and care for 'people' who make a community.

'Community' was born when the world and humanity were created. Genesis 1:26 reads: "Then God said, "Let us make man in our image, in our likeness and let them rule over the fish of the sea and the birds of the air, over the livestock, over all the earth and over all the creatures that move along the ground" (NIV). The personal plural pronoun "us" that God referred to is something to reflect on. It was not just God-Me who was singular but it was God-Us who was plural who created the world and the humanity. In the beginning, God-Community was very present. The Hebrew word for God is *elohiym*, which is a plural noun. Doctrinally, it was God-Trinity, Three-in-One, the Father, the Son, the Holy Spirit. The United Methodist Church believes that "in unity of this Godhead

147

there are three persons, of one substance, power and eternity—the Father, the Son, and the Holy Ghost" as per the Articles of Religion of The United Methodist Church.[1] God-Us, God-Community, and Godhead are the key for our faith and ministry. When man and woman were created, they were created in the image and likeness of God-Community, which means, a sense of community was imparted into humanity right from day one. Therefore, humanity as a 'community' was an integral part of God-Community's plan, purpose and will.

When the call of God-Community came to Abram (Gen. 12:2-5), the manifold blessing included all communities on earth being blessed through Abram. When his name was changed from Abraham, he became father of many nations—people groups and communities. The name Abram means father of one and that's Ishmael through Hagar. After establishing and confirming a covenant between God-Community and Abram, he could not stay as father of one but had to become father of many and more. God told Abram: "I am [God-Community] Almighty. . . . No longer will you be called Abram; your name will be Abraham, for I have made you a father of many nations . . . I will make you very fruitful" (Gen. 17:1, 5-6, NIV). God-Community called Abraham to be a keeper of a covenant and to be fruitful. Abraham is commonly known as the father of the faithful, the pioneer of our faith movement, and the adventurer among the patriarchs. Today, three major religious communities—Judaism, Islam, and Christianity—revere him as their father.

When the call of God-Community came to Jacob (Gen. 32), the grandson of Abraham, Jacob's name was changed from to "Israel." God-Community wrestled with Jacob all through a night when Jacob was confused, perplexed, and fearful. Again, it was *elohiym* who appeared to Jacob and transformed him, not just with a name change, but with the birth of a community called "the people of Israel." The Hebrew name *Israel* means "striver with God." Jacob struggled, contended, labored hard and eventually surrendered himself to the extent that he became a vehicle through which a community of God's called-out people was birthed. He named the place "Peniel," which in Hebrew means "face of *elohiym*." He saw the face of God-Community. Then, he received a great promise: "I am God Almighty; be fruitful and increase in number. A nation and a community of nations will come from you, and kings will come from your body." (Gen. 35:11). The word *community* in Hebrew language is *qahal*, one of the most important masculine plural nouns in the entire Old Testament. It occurs 103 times in the Hebrew Old Testament. It means a convocation, a congregation, an assembly, a crowd, a multitude, an army, a gathering, and a community. It is important to know that the Greek Septuagint usually translates *qahal* with *ekklesia*, which is a common term for a congregation, the called-out people or the people of new Israel, the church.

In the New Testament, the word *ekklesia* is used to denote both local community in a particular area and the whole people of God on earth. It occurs 115 times (Luke, 24 times; John, 20 times; Matthew, 3 times; Paul, 68 times). In the New Testament period, *ekklesia* was used for a faith community of Christians who met in a house of worship and edification. In the early chapters of Acts, the Christians are described as disciples, saints, brothers and sisters, believers and followers of Jesus Christ. In Pauline writings, Jesus Christ is depicted as the Head of the Church and the relationship is of Head to Body. In others words, Paul brings out this truth—almost in every epistle—that Christ is the head of *ekklesia*. Here is a great affirmation of the Second-Person in God-Community or Trinity leading the Faith Community, which began from a band of disciples who became the nucleus of the "New Israel." We call it *church*, which is essentially people of all ages, nations, and races throughout the world. This clearly indicates that we did not create the church by our efforts but simply received it as a gift from God-Community and also have become part of the faith community, purely and solely by God's grace and guidance.

Membership is not by human appointment but by Divine call. Therefore, it is a blessed community of faith-driven and grace-filled people gathered by God-Community through Christ. The church, the Faith Community, belongs to God-Community because He is the One who has called it into being, dwells in it, and realizes His purpose through it. The faith community is the agent of God's mission on earth as per the Great Commandment—Love God-Community; Love People (of all nations and races)—and the Great Commission—Go (to all communities), Preach, Baptize, Teach. The promise to Abraham and Israel is fulfilled through the faith community. Moreover, the faith community is the means of God's transforming grace to the world. It is a channel of God's blessings of help, hope and healing to the world. In this sense, the faith community is a sacrament to the world with its prayers, presence, gifts, service and witness. The faith community, traditionally called "the Church" exists for the sole benefit of all people of the world because of the simple but powerful statement of Jesus: "God so loved the world" (John 3:16). The same Jesus said later in his ministry time: "I will build my church" (Matt. 16:18). Putting those statements together, it is crystal clear that Jesus intended the church, the faith community, to be the means of God's love to all people of the world. Every faith community is called, expected, and mandated to be present in the community to share the good news of Jesus Christ and to bring all people from darkness to light, from sin to salvation, and from death to life. The faith community was born on the Day of Pentecost for the missional purpose of embracing the global community, fulfilling the promise of God to Abraham and Israel, the prophetic words of Jesus to his disciples, and the passionate statement of John Wesley, "The world is [and will be] my [our] parish."

The Features or Distinctives of the First Faith Community

The first feature or distinctive was the empowering ministry of the Holy Spirit. Undoubtedly, the Day of Pentecost was, is, and will be one of the greatest days in the history of the *ekklesia*. The Holy Spirit fell upon ordinary people of color from diverse cultures and contexts who became extraordinary people doing extraordinary things in an extraordinary way. They spoke in different languages, a clear prophetic sign that the gospel would reach every people group in line with the Great Commandment and the Great Commission. Until Pentecost, it was a Jewish mandate, and now the Holy Spirit empowered the first faith community to bring Gentiles into the *ekklesia*. In Acts 10, this is shown through a powerful vision of a sheet letting down from heaven and a clear voice telling Peter to get up and to kill and eat. Peter was exhorted to kill, meaning to stop the spirit of exclusion and to eat, meaning to embrace people of all nations and races with a spirit of inclusion. In the Kingdom-Community, no one is forbidden. If Christianity had ended with four gospels, it would have been a gospel without diversity and dynamism. The Spirit-empowered community was able to turn the world upside down.

The second feature or distinctive was devotion to be a learning community. The early faith community gave their unattended attention to the apostles' teaching of how to love God-Community passionately and how to love all community people missionally so that the first faith community would become a beloved global community. Using the power of imagination, I believe, 3,000 new disciples gathered Sunday after Sunday in Solomon's Colonnade to worship and to learn about loving God passionately. During the week days, they broke into small groups and gathered in groups at homes to study and to learn about building interpersonal relationships with one another. They were growing in loving relationships both vertically and horizontally. *Agape* for God and with people brought new converts, and led them to rejoice in their salvation and to fellowship with other believers. Above all, the first missionary journey took off when the first faith community was growing organically and steadily. Their daily prayer was: Give us a teachable and responsive spirit that we may continue to stay a beloved community.

The third feature or distinctive was a deep of sense of community and fellowship. The Greek word for *fellowship* is *koinonia*, which is translated as "community." Prior to Pentecost, there was no real sense of fellowship among God's people. There was no deep sense of unity and oneness. C.H. Dodd, a Greek scholar, points out, "The noun *koinonia* means "fellowship," and another noun is *koinonos* which means "partner" and the verb *koinonos* means "to share."[2] These meanings indicate: (1) We live together as one family or one community; (2) We have things in common; (3) We are shareholders in a common concern; (4) We share everything God wants us to share; (5) We believe the same God who lives in me lives in others; (6) We believe the same Jesus who has saved me can save all people; (7) We believe the same Spirit who energies my life can also energize all people; (8) We believe we are called to do something for Jesus with what we have in common; (9) We share in so that we may share out with those in need; (10) We belong to one another; we affect one another; we need one another; This sense of community and fellowship led the people of the first *ekklesia* to be a people of caring. When a severe famine was predicted for Jerusalem and the entire Roman world, the church at Antioch decided to provide help for the people living in Judea.

The fourth feature or distinctive was a clear sense of the worth of every person—no class or racial barriers. Acts 13:1 reports, "In the church at Antioch there were prophets and teachers: Barnabas, Simeon called Niger, Lucius of Cyrene, Manaen (who had been brought up with Herod the Tetrarch) and Saul" (NIV). In this verse, the author Luke intentionally lists the names in this order. Barnabas is named first and Saul last. In the middle is a man by the name of Manaen, who, in the words of the translator Moffatt, was a foster brother of Herod the tetrarch. Then comes Simeon from North Africa and then at the end Saul. Eventually, Saul and Barnabas were commissioned to preach the gospel to the Gentiles by Simeon and Manaen, one from Africa and another from a palace. This indicates that the *ekklesia* at Antioch was emerging as classless and free of racial prejudice. If the church had remained that way throughout its history, then it would have made a much greater impact upon the world. Andrew Walls puts it: "To make distinctions between people based on the color of their skin is to introduce into the Body of Christ a foreign substance which will fester and poison the whole Body."[3] If and when the faith community is filled with any distinction then it is emptied of Christ because "there is neither Jew nor Greek, slave nor free, male nor female, for you are all one in Christ Jesus," (Gal 3:28, NIV).

The fifth feature or distinctive was unbroken unity and fellowship in the midst of disagreements. In Acts 6, we are told the Grecian Jews were complaining about their widows not being treated well in the daily distribution of food. In Acts 11, we are told of the record of doctrinal issues around circumcision and the disagreements between Jewish Christians and Gentile Christians. In Acts 15, we are told of a sharp disagreement between Paul and Barnabas over the issues related to John Mark, another missionary from the mission tour of Asia. The first faith community leaders who were the apostles of the day dealt with each situation with grace and confidence. They did not sweep them under the carpet, nor did they ignore them. They acted promptly with lots of prayer that the faith community was saved. The leaders let the *ekklesia* be open and receptive to the work of the Holy Spirit, who was not just present but also moving among them day in and day out. When Paul and Barnabas decided to part ways, they did so gracefully and faithfully without losing the focus on the mission of the church. Peter, Paul, Barnabas, John Mark, and Silas approached every such situation with forgiveness, reconciliation, cordiality, maturity, faithfulness, and above all with a plan of restorative justice, filled with the Spirit, taken up with Christ, and committed to moving forward.

The Global Missional Faith Community

From the faith of Abraham to the Pauline theology of *ekklesia*, the single golden thread or strand is God-Community's deep desire for all peoples, tribes, and nations to come into His Kingdom. The *ekklesia* can't have an authentic theology without a compelling vision and contemporary engagement in mission to all the peoples. Abraham had planted the seed of faith in God's mission of being "a blessing" to "all the peoples," which got multiplied and culminated in the churches or faith communities that Paul preached to and planted. In A.D. 37, most Christians were Jews. At that time, Jerusalem was not only the main Christian center, Jerusalem Christians also laid down the norms, rules, and standards for other Christians. By A.D. 325, few Christians were Jews and the main Christian centers were located in the Eastern Mediterranean. The key language for Christians was Greek. By A.D. 600, the balance completely shifted westward and the growing edge of Christianity was among the northern and western tribal and semi-tribal people, and Ireland was a power center. In the 1840s, Great Britain became a prominent Christian nation with the vision of expanding the gospel to the world. Since 1980, the balance has shifted south, and the continents of Africa and South America are currently becoming notable for their numbers of those who profess Christian faith and call themselves Christians. It's no longer a community of faith "within" but a community faith "throughout." The gospel of Jesus Christ was intended to belong to people of all nations and races, every nation, every race, and every tribe. One nation or one tribe or one race cannot set the standards and make decisions for all because all nations, races, and tribes have direct connection to the Savior and to the Christian Scriptures. God-Community intervened in history and opened the door wide and broad for all people to have a place to feel at home. The golden thread that connects the Bible and today's church is the joy of being in the mission of God-Community that all the peoples, not only one race or one community, are welcomed, embraced, accepted, and celebrated. Exodus 22:21 tells us, "Do not mistreat an alien or oppress anyone, for you were aliens in Egypt" (NIV). This was the law for all the children of Abraham.

The Global Missional Faith Community continues to expand by reaching out to people of every nation, race, and ethnic group because of specific *missional reasons*. The first and foremost reason is its focus on people and "all the peoples" regardless of color, caste and creed. The Reformers of the seventeenth and eighteenth centuries emphasized as the "marks of the true church" that such a church exists wherever the gospel is preached, the sacraments rightly administered, and church discipline exercised. This understanding gives the impression that a church is a place where certain things happen and people "go to church." The Reformers' view does not reflect the community's role as the bearer of missional responsibility throughout the world near and far: to take the Gospel to people. If the goal is simply getting people to go to church, the results are predictable: the same people go to church and the same activities happen Sunday after Sunday. There is no creativity and no diversity. If, however, "church" goes to "people," the approach becomes theocentric, stressing that the mission of God for all peoples is the foundation for the mission of the Church. God sent His Son into the world; God did not just invite the world to the Son.

The second missional reason is the proclamation of the gospel to all peoples. The gospel is the good news of and about Jesus Christ—his life, ministry, death, and resurrection. "Christ has died; Christ is risen; Christ will come again." Also, the gospel is about what Jesus preached, taught and did during his earthly ministry. If what we proclaim about Christ is not a reflection of the gospel that he preached and taught, then we are not doing justice to the proclamation. All of Jesus' preaching, teaching, and miracle-performance were about the Kingdom of God that included the challenge to discipleship, ethical teaching, forgiveness of sins, and the welcoming of the outcast in the name of God-Community into the faith community. When Jesus sent out his disciples, he commanded them to preach and demonstrate the Kingdom of God, which was and is for individuals and for community. Church people often think about how to get people into the church, whereas kingdom people think and plan about how to get the church to all peoples. Church people worry about the world changing the church, whereas kingdom people envision transformation of all peoples. The evangel is God-Community's good news of liberation, of restoration, of wholeness, and of salvation that is personal, social, global, and cosmic.

The third missional reason is community-building. Jesus' parable on two builders (see Matt. 7:24-27; Luke 6:47-49) reminds us clearly that the *ekklesia* is in the business of building up, not breaking down. The questions are: Where do we build? What do we build with? How do we build? Why do we build? Every church is called to build on rock; when it fails to do so it risks becoming a victim of storms. Every church is called to build the community within and the community outside; those who fail to do so risk losing their identity as Kingdom People. The most significant thing that makes the difference is the foundation. One man built his house on sand and the other on rock. The figure of speech here is very simple. The secret of building a strong foundation is to hear and heed the words of Jesus. In Matthew, the parable is located in the last section of the Sermon on the Mount, inviting us is to appropriate what we need from the context of chapters 5–7 because of the conjunction "therefore." Jesus talked about many things in those chapters that are the materials to be used for building the foundation. Every faith community is called to be salt and light, to control their thoughts, to fulfill the law, to avoid anger, to give to the needy, to pray regularly, and to stop worrying. These are the materials to be used for the business of building communities that are strong and stable.

The fourth missional reason is Christian service to all peoples, based on their spiritual, emotional, mental, social, family, and physical needs. John 13:5 reads: "Jesus poured water into a basin and began to wash his disciples' feet" (NIV) Dr. Alexander Maclaren stated "The greatest truths are not just spoken but acted."[4] He went on to illustrate the point by referring to Mary of Bethany who broke the alabaster box of ointment; she spoke no eloquent words but performed a most eloquent deed. And when the faith community takes bread and wine or juice, little is said but a lot is acted. This reflects the powerful words of the hymn: "Jesu, Jesu, fill us with your love, show us how to serve the neighbors we have from you."[5] Because Jesus served, today we have the gift of salvation. When the faith community focuses on how we can serve others then they are truly, very truly, demonstrating follower-ship. The Greek word *diakonia* is used in the New Testament for ministry and the meaning of this word is "service;" that's putting oneself at others' disposal to give whatever help the faith community can offer in Christian love. Mark 10:45 reads, "The Son of Man also came not to be served but to serve" (NIV). The very purpose of His coming into the world was to serve all peoples by healing the sick, feeding the hungry, redeeming the demon-possessed, giving sight to the blind, teaching, and counseling with compassion and love.

Diverse Communities as God's Design and Purpose

God has gifted the world with families, communities, cultures, and races as a blessing and also to be a blessing. God is glorified and magnified when diverse people groups come together, work together, worship together, and serve together as one family of God-Community. The Lord Jesus commissioned his followers to make disciples of all nations. They were to be witnesses in Jerusalem, and in all Judea and Samaria, and to the ends of the earth. He promised them the Holy Spirit to empower and guide them. On the Day of Pentecost, the spectacular event was the birth of the Faith Community that was deeply committed to take the gospel from local to global so that Christ was made available to all peoples.

The origin of peoples and the diversity of cultures and races continue to be part of God-Community's creation and His will. The good news is that its future is eternal. The diversity will never be replaced by uniformity. Acts 17:26 reads, "He made from one every nation of mankind to live on all the face of the earth, having determined their appointed times and the boundaries of their habitation" (NIV). The word *nation* is *ethnos* or *ethne* in Greek, which means people or ethnic group. This means that the origin of people groups is not in spite of, but because of God's creative will and plan. He also set them in their places or locations. The diversity is

God's idea. The missional call or the missional task is rooted in the very purpose of God-Community. The idea of diversity is not temporary; it is determined for eternity, from the Garden of Eden to the new heaven and earth, where people will gather from every tribe, every tongue, every ethnic group, and every nation. According to John the author of the book of Revelation, diversity will not disappear but always finds a permanent place in the Kingdom of God both now and forever.

There is always beauty and power of praise when diverse communities gather in the presence of the Lord. The analogy is of a choir that sings in parts, which brings more beauty than the choir singing in unison. Unity in diversity is more beautiful and more powerful than the unity of uniformity. "Declare his glory among the nations, his marvelous works among all the peoples! For great is the Lord and greatly to be praised" (Ps. 96:3-4, NIV). By focusing on all the people groups of the world, God puts His amazing grace upon all peoples, which means God does not choose one people group because of any distinctive of worth, but rather that all people groups become a means of bringing other groups into the Kingdom of God. The ultimate goal of God-Community is the missional focus of advancing His purpose through the gift of diversity.

Caste System in Indian Church, Context and Culture

India (which is my mother land) is a land of many cultures, languages, and ethnic groups. It is a multinational state with a federation of cultures. There are many nations in one country. India represents a baffling variety with 1,652 languages (mother tongues). There are official languages (meaning approved by the federal government), major languages, and minor languages. Apart from language, India is a land of many religions. Another way of understanding India is in terms of people groups—castes, tribes, and ethno-linguistic groups. The Anthropological Survey of India estimated 4,635 communities or people groups in India. A people group is defined as people having common affinity or bond or likeness for one another because of their shared language, religion, ethnicity, residence, occupation, class or caste, situation, or a combination of these. One very predominant feature of Indian culture is the caste system that has its root in Hinduism. There are four basic castes that have originated from the body of god: *Brahmins* from mouth or head, *Ksatriya* from arms or chest, *Vaisya* from thighs or waist, and *Sudra* from the feet. *Brahmins* are the rulers, the guardians, the dispensers of divine power, the teachers of Hindu Scriptures, and they claim to be the high caste. *Ksatriyas* are the soldiers, the protectors, and they claim to be the upper middle caste. *Vaisyas* represent different professionals such as traders, farmers, cattle tenders, and teachers, and they claim to be the middle caste. *Sudras* are the menial job workers or servants, who are considered the low caste. The *adivasis* or tribals are outside these caste groups, and they claim to be the "original dwellers" of the land.

The Brahmins are declared to be chief because they were created from the mouth (of God), punning on the word *mukha* that means mouth or chief. They represent the profession of the poet-priest, the most privileged position in the society or the highest caste. Their function is to teach and officiate at sacrifices, and their aim is to be preeminent in sacred knowledge. The priest's profession is hereditary. Only they have knowledge about God, and they are expected to speak about the truth. Thus, they become the indispensable mediators in all the important events of both private and public life. They can do only what is right and perfect. They also have an absolute monopoly over all higher education because they are regarded as the most literate group in the society.

The Hindu charismatic leaders, including Ram Mohan Roy, Keshub Chandra Sen, and Swami Vivekananda, disapproved of the caste system. They removed the "sacred thread" meant for the upper caste as a sign of renouncing their caste. Keshub Chandra Sen went to the extent of encouraging inter-caste marriages. They all attempted to bring socio-religious reformation. The religious-political leaders such as Mahatma Gandhi said that untouchability is a cancer, and it is a breach of the doctrine of *ahimsa*, which means nonviolence. They campaigned against such a system in the society. The traditional philosophers, such as S. Radhakrishnan, suggested improving the Hindu social life by getting rid of castes and sub-castes, by removing untouchability, and by extending initiation of Vedic studies to all Hindus, without any distinction of caste, sex, or creed. Spiritual heritage should be made available to all Hindus. The Hindu prophetic personalities, such as Sri Aurobindo Ghose and Rabindranath Tagore, also did not approve the caste hierarchy; they promote brotherhood, national integration, and communal harmony.

Every human being is part of at least ethnic, sex, and age categories. In the context of missional strategy, missiologists (see especially Donald McGavran) accepted different castes as people groups. McGavran said: "The Bible itself authorizes a discipling of the many peoples of the world without destroying these peoples, these minorities, *ethne*, castes and tribes."[6] People group churches are strong and stable as they continue normal relationships among the members of the group, under the local leadership of the village. They work together as a strong community in the church as they are interrelated. The decisions are collectively done so they stand firm together even at times of crisis and persecution. People group movement produces strong indigenous local leadership that has access to the entire group. When such leaders are identified and trained, they become effective leaders in the local churches. They are able to love people, as most of them are related to those they serve. People group churches can easily become self-supporting, as together they make decisions to construct their own church building and extend ministry support to the church leader willingly and generously. People contribute their labor or something in kind for any church-related manual work. People begin to share about their new faith with their relatives in other villages or places, in a natural way without any fear. Often group conversion gives religious authenticity that is a positive factor for evangelism, with less chance of opposition and persecution. When fellowship and moral support are available for one another in the group, ex-communication from the village or group is not possible. People group movement results in rapid growth of the church. The local faith community grows and also produces daughter churches in other locations.

Developing Cross-Cultural and Cross-Racial Ministries

One of the effective ways to confront issues such as castism and racism is to intentionally explore cross-cultural and cross-racial ministries. When the *ekklesia* is faced with barriers such as culture, race, caste, religion, and language, there needs to be a missional approach or solution by taking the barriers and turning them into opportunities for creative ministries. Cross-cultural and cross-racial ministries are not only the crucial immediate need but also the biblical mandate. The Bible takes note of both cultural differences and distances. In Acts 1:8, Jesus referred his disciples to the worldwide scope of God-Community's concern—"in Jerusalem, in all Judea, and in Samaria, and unto the uttermost part of the earth" (NIV). If it were not for this verse, the gospel would not have gone to the five continents. There would not even be the World Council of Churches, World Methodist Council, World Vision, Compassion International, General Board of Global Ministries, and many other worldwide mission organizations. Jesus, in this verse, did not merely talk about geographical distance but about cultural distance between Jerusalem and Judea, Jerusalem and Samaria, Jerusalem and the rest of the world. Jesus also implied the need to missionally and evangelistically address the walls of prejudice. Jesus challenged his disciples to strategically cross the boundary by involving the local culture and language, taking the water of life in an indigenized cup.

There are a few principles to be proactively considered for developing cross-cultural and cross-racial ministries. The first principle is to have a global vision. Where there is no vision, people perish, and where there is vision, people thrive. Vision is the driving force for all and every creative ministry of the faith communities. George Barna defines vision as "the clear mental image of a preferable future, imparted by God to his chosen servants, based on accurate understanding of God, yourself and your circumstances."[7] God is a missionary God because He sent His only Son. Every Christian is a missionary because he or she is sent into all peoples. The circumstances include the immediate critical need of moving from monoculture to multiculture and multicultural ministries. Vision gives direction and focus. Vision is like a magnifying glass. In the beginning, it looks small because it has not become reality, but vision makes it bigger and faith increases. Vision is also like a telescope, an instrument that helps to see objects from a distance. Vision can create excitement because the reality has been seen mentally but it is a matter of time to celebrate the adventure. Vision determines where the faith community is going. It helps the leadership to set goals or objectives. It keeps the church moving by creating momentum. William Carey, the father of the modern missionary movement has said, "Expect great things from God and attempt great things for God."[8]

The second principle is the power of prayer. Prayer is the lifeline of the faith community, because it is the primary source of church health and growth. When there is more prayer, there will be more power. There is a great lesson to learn from the South Korean churches about prayer. The pastor of the largest church in the world says, "He prays, listens and obeys."[9] His prayer is growing the church, and the people's prayers keep the pastor praying. The Prayer Mountain of the largest Methodist church in the world is another example for church growth through prayer.[10] Prayer and growth are two sides of a coin. Prayer needs to become the topmost priority in the life of every faith community. When God is willing to hear and to answer all the prayers, according to His promises, there should not be any hurdle to pray. There is a universal saying, "prayers go up and blessings come down." In Luke 19:46, we know that Jesus called the temple as a house of prayer. Every faith community is a house of prayer, not just in name but in reality. In order to grow an outward mission focus, every faith community must dedicate themselves to personal and corporate spiritual disciplines, if they intend to increase their participation in God's global cause.

The third principle is the empowerment of leaders. Many writers have focused on gifts that empower the people of God to serve. Without the gifts of the Spirit, the church becomes something quite different from what God had originally intended, as the church is called to be an organism. The faith community needs to realize that it is the body of Christ, and the mission of Jesus Christ can be fulfilled only with diverse gifts and diverse people. The early church grew rapidly because the new converts were taught that the Holy Spirit imparted not only salvation experience but also spiritual gifts. They were responsible to discover, develop, and exercise them. Paul writes to the Corinthian believers, "to each is given the manifestation of the Spirit for the common good" (1 Cor. 12:7, NIV). Peter writes, "Like good stewards of the manifold grace of God, serve one another with whatever gift each of you has received" (1 Peter 4:10, NIV). God gave different gifts so the community would be involved in different ministries, especially developing cross-cultural and cross-racial ministries and meeting the needs of people within and outside. When God sees the faith community faithfully exercising their gifts, He grows the ministries in and outside the church.

The fourth principle is leadership development in the area of multicultural ministries. This dynamic is crucial for all effective ministries, especially for developing and planting cross-cultural and cross-racial ministries and faith communities. Both clergy and laity are to be adequately equipped to fulfill this mission. Leaders of the church growth (people) movement continue to teach that a healthy multiethnic church is a church that encourages, motivates, and equips clergy and laity of the church. Every local church is called to nourish, train, and uphold its members for the ministries in the world, especially in the arts of hospitality, generosity, integration, and the spirit of discernment and inclusion. *Discipleship* can be defined as "participation in lifelong learning and servanthood." Jesus was interested primarily in having, not crowds, but disciples in whom and through whom His ministry would be multiplied many times over. The church is called to meet the world with trained people. Every congregation needs to see the significant importance for men and women to be trained in the area of their giftedness. The first priority of a pastor is to invest in people so that they become disciples first and then ministers of Jesus Christ.

The fifth principle is commitment to evangelism. In a country like United States of America, if the church is to grow cross-racially and multiculturally, evangelism is not an option but a necessity. Evangelism is the duty of the whole church. It is the duty of each member, whatever age or background or caste or race he or she belongs to. For doing evangelism, one need not be educationally or theologically qualified or competent. It is simply presenting Jesus Christ as an answer for all the needs of humanity or for a particular individual, community, or group. People crave results, hope, and concrete solutions. The message is simple that Jesus Christ, the unique person, can help anyone to find hope for all the storms of life. Evangelism is also a lifestyle. When the unique person is introduced, people must see the reflection of His life and ministry in the word and the deed of the one who provides the introduction. It has been said, "Evangelism is love in action." People are carefully watching Christianity, Christians, and Churches.

The sixth principle is an attitude of service with love and compassion. Francis Xavier is one of my favorite (Roman Catholic) missionaries to India, who helps me understand the Meta-Church model. He was greatly influenced by Ignatius Loyola, who founded the Society of Jesus. He committed to become a lifelong missionary, taking the gospel to the poor and the sick in some of the remotest parts of the world. During the Portuguese period (1500–1700), Francis Xavier arrived in India, having traveled for eleven months, as a representative of the Pope. He began his missionary work during his travels, ministering to seasick persons; and therefore the passengers considered him a saint. He began his ministry in a Union Territory of India known as the island of Goa. Today it is a Roman Catholic place, claiming to have preserved the body of Xavier, which is open to the public once every ten years. The Church of Francis Xavier is one of the historical monuments in India. He began his ministry through Christian Education/ Training among youth and children, teaching them moral and spiritual values. He reached adults through youth and children. Then, he concentrated in the east coastal area, among one people/caste group, called paravas, who are fishermen by profession, spread among thirty villages. According to his diary, Francis Xavier baptized 11,000 persons in just one day. Today there are 700,000 Roman Catholic fishermen and women in that area because of his ministry. He learned the local language within a short period and translated much Christian literature. He appointed local leaders and left a book of Christian education in every village for training purposes. He also went to Malaga, Indonesia, and Japan for missionary work. He very much desired to go to China where no missionary had yet gone, but he could go only to the border, six miles from China, where he died because of over travel and exhaustion. Francis Xavier had a big vision and bigger dream, and therefore he had the biggest harvest in and around India. The Meta-Church model is a model for church growth in this century, applicable both here and everywhere in the world. From Xavier's letters to various local leaders, several church-growth principles have emerged:

- Be conscious of your personal life and your relationship with your God, because your neighbors will have to learn from your life;
- Lead a simple life;
- Be humble and try to grow in humility;
- Meet and pray for every sick person in your village;
- Help all the poor under your care;
- Preach the word at all situations and opportunities and to all people groups;
- Speak clearly and avoid doctrinal disputes;
- Train people in such a way that they learn to grow in maturity;
- Encourage every Christian to serve God and people.[11]

The seventh principle is contextualization. The methods used to develop multicultural and multiracial congregations have to fit the context. One size does not fit all because contexts are very different. Contexts include demographics, community profiles, global mindset, and a healthy environment for growth and kingdom potential. Some people are mature, ready and ripe to learn, and they take off in their global vision and mission. Some may be advanced in their understanding and thinking but not sharing the common vision and mission because they are stuck in a local mindset. Educating people in global vision and mission involves a thorough process. It's a long journey requiring patience and perseverance. To be effective in getting the core group of people or leaders intentionally engaged, it is critically important to listen to their past stories, present needs, and future hopes. People cannot be forced to get involved in global vision. Embracing people of different cultures, races, castes, and colors has to emerge from God-Community's call and people's commitment to building a Beloved Community. Therefore, the best way or method is to continue to educate, equip, empower, and enable and to leave the rest in the hands of God Almighty. Therefore, it is very important to listen and find out the contextual needs from people groups and move into planning and strategizing for creative multiracial, caste, color, and culture ministries. An effective mobilizer always seeks new and better ways to share and to implement global mission and vision.

Building Bricks of Beloved Community

Building a beloved community is not a utopia but a hope, a challenge, an opportunity, a ministry, and a possibility. The first brick is compassion. Becoming a people of mercy, forgiveness, and healthy relationships is not only good for our lives but also for the global community, especially in countries where poverty and sickness are rapidly increasing. We are called to act with justice; we are called to love tenderly; we are called to serve one another; we are called to walk humbly with God according to the prophet Micah (6:8). Jesus prescribed a (ever) lasting medicine for shalom in the world. God is merciful. Deuteronomy 4:31 reads: "For the LORD your God is a merciful God" (NIV). In spite of disobedience, idolatry, and awful deeds of the people of Israel, God continued to remind them of His faithfulness to the covenant based on mercy.

My favorite author and Christian counselor, Selwyn Hughes. makes an interesting distinction between grace and mercy. *Grace* is getting something you don't deserve; *mercy* is not getting something you do deserve. Grace is especially associated with people in their sins; mercy is especially associated with people in their misery. Grace looks down upon sin and seeks to save; mercy looks especially upon the miserable consequences of sin and seeks to relieve. The parable of the Good Samaritan is an apt illustration for what mercy looks like. The Samaritan was compassionate and did something about it. In other words, he translated compassion into action, taking the injured man to a motel and making provisions for his healing and recovery.

The second brick is forgiveness. Someone said, "I love mankind—it is people I can't stand." In the Old Testament, forgiveness is spoken of as "pardon" and "covering." God does not remember our sins because He has covered them. The focus is just God's forgiveness. In the New Testament, Jesus teaches us to pray, "Forgive us our debts, as we also have forgiven our debtors" (Matt. 6:2, NIV). Jesus widened the spectrum of forgiveness by teaching His disciples that if and when we expect God to forgive us then we must be willing to forgive our family members, church members, friends, coworkers, and neighbors. "To err is human, to forgive is divine." The focus is both God's forgiveness and human forgiveness, one leading the other. The parable in Matthew 18 on "forgiveness" is given in answer to a question by Peter, "'How often shall I forgive my brother [or sister]? Up to seven times?' Jesus answered, 'I tell you, not seven times, but seventy-seven times'" (18:21-22, NIV). Then He continued the discourse on forgiveness by telling them a story. The bottom line of the story is that the master forgave one of his servants, whereas the servant did not forgive one of his colleagues or co-servants. We are called and commissioned as a community of forgiving people so that we might become a community accepting all people so that we might become a beloved community.

The third brick is healing. The global community, in many ways, is broken, and people are going through distress. Rather than rejoicing, people are pushed into a time of feeling saddened because they not only feel the loss of something but also they feel excluded, discriminated against, and exploited. They cause pain. Pain causes hurts and injuries. This is a psychological problem because emotions are involved. Grief, sorrow, anger, and sadness are taking away from being and becoming a beloved community. People don't have any value for maturing in faith or enhancing ministries. Therefore, we are invited to make a "brick" called "healing and reconciliation" so that we become aware of our pain and begin to draw strength and power from the cross, the empty tomb, and the day of Pentecost to deal with it. God's comfort cannot fully reach us until we are real people. When we are willing to accept and acknowledge our pain of being excluded and to seek help, hope, and healing, then transformation happens through healing and restoration. Then we become what Henri Nouwen named God's people, "wounded healers." Without being healed by the power of God's love, we cannot project ourselves as sources of God's healing to the broken and hurting world. A Christian is one who is cared for, healed, and comforted by the power of God's love for the sole purpose of caring for, healing, comforting, and reconciling with others.

The fourth brick is the gifts of all people. The book *Eighth Day of Creation* includes an apocryphal story. Michael Angelo was pushing a large hunk of stone down the street toward his sculpting studio when a neighbor cried out, "Hey, Michael, what are you going to do with that old piece of stone?" Michael replied, "There is an angel in there that wants to come out."[12] There is an angel that can come out of every believer or member of the faith community. This totally challenges the myth that only certain categories of people have gifts, especially when it comes to leadership positions. God-Community is the One who gives the spiritual gifts that are to be discovered, developed, and deployed. Those who read this book, congratulations! You are gifted. Some are chosen to be apostles, prophets, evangelists, pastors (through ordination/commissioning), and teachers. God-Community-given gifts are intended for the building up of the body of Christ. They are all gifts of the divine grace. The grace of God is the reason for these gifts. One of the favorite slogans of John Wesley was "Grace in all and grace for all." Wesley was an apostle, a prophet, an evangelist, a pastor, and a teacher. The word *charis* for "grace" means that all believers have gifts, without exception. The early church began to grow rapidly because when converts were immediately taught that the Holy Spirit was imparted in him or her not only for salvation experience but also equipped him or her with a spiritual gift. That person was responsible to discover, develop, and deploy the gift in the local faith community. Diverse people with diverse gifts make a beloved community. Thanks be to God, God-Community is delighted.

The fifth brick is *agape*. What the twenty-first century faith community needs is to learn about loving relationships the exact way as Jesus loved and as Paul taught. Love #1: deep affection and warm feeling for another; love #2: the emotion of romance that includes the strong need for another; love #3: strong fondness or enthusiasm for an idea, person, place, or thing; love #4: God's benevolence toward humanity. Paul, in his first letter to the Corinthian church, explains the ideals of *agape*, or God's love or Christian love. Verses 4-7 show that love is patient with others (especially difficult people), kind to others, does not envy others, does not boast before others, and is not proud or rude to others or self-seeking at the expense of others. Love keeps no record of the wrongs of others. Love does not delight in evil, but rejoices in truth. Love always protects those who are oppressed and exploited, trusts all peoples, hopes for all peoples, and perseveres with all peoples. Love never fails anyone. Agape love is a difficult practice. It takes intentional and careful efforts, of course with God's help, to put away all enmity and hatred toward others. It also takes courage and strength to be generous in our love, meekness, mercy, and grace toward all peoples because agape love is God's love to us and then to others. His love is manifested toward all people. God loves us, and we commit to love Him and to show His love to others—people of all ages, nations, and races.

The sixth brick is hope. There is a troublesome emotion that can arise in the human heart called despair. The dictionary defines despair as "the loss of hope, the refusal to struggle, a deadening of the heart to the idea that one will be helped or rescued."[13] We continue to struggle with difficult emotions—abandonment, isolation, rejection, and psychological pain that eventually leads us to despair. Psychologists claim that when tracing despair to its source, they find it comes from emptiness. The loss of hope is one of the worst things that can happen to God's people spiritually. When we are troubled by relational, social, mental, and racial problems and difficulties, we can go on because hope fills our hearts and minds and souls with a message that things will change for the better. That's why, someone said, "Hope is the memory of the future." Hope sustains us by holding out the promise of better days ahead. The famous painting called "Hope" by the artist G. F. Watts shows a blindfolded woman sitting on a sphere with a bowed head, and in her hands she holds a lyre. Only one string of the instrument remains unbroken. Only one star shines in the dark sky. The message of the painting is that as long as there is one star in the sky and one string on the instrument, there is hope. As long as there is God-Community, who is Emanuel—God with us, there is hope always. There is always a balm in Gilead to make the wounded whole and to heal the sin-sick soul. The good news is that we are not alone. God-Community is with us, and we are with God's people who are the stars in the dark sky and strings of the instrument. The stars, as they did for the magi, will lead us into the bright presence of God-Community. The music from the strings, as they did for David, will make us feel better. It takes time for us to gain our spiritual equilibrium to know that even though we can't hold onto God-Community, He is faithful in holding on to us. That's the vision of God-Community with hope.

Conclusion

In his plenary speech at the General Conference of the Methodist Church in India (November 15, 1989), Bishop James K. Matthews shared that a missionary to India talked with Mahatma Gandhi and put to him a question: "What should we Christians do to help the men and women of India?" Gandhi replied: "I would suggest four things. First of all, all Christians and missionaries must begin to live more like Jesus Christ. Second, that you practice your religion without adulterating it or toning it down. Third, that you emphasize love and make it your working force, for love is central in Christianity. Fourth, that you study the non-Christian religions more sympathetically so that you can have a more sympathetic approach to people."[14] What Gandhi was saying, quite simply, is that if you want to be valid and authentic, then be more like your Master. Be Christian. Therefore, let us commit ourselves to draw strength from God-Community—Father, Son, and Holy Spirit—and build a beloved community for now and for eternity.

Notes

1. *The Book of Discipline of The United Methodist Church* (Nashville: The United Methodist Church, 2008), para. 103, article I.Mark Deymas, Building a Healthy Multi-Ethnic Church.

2. Dodd, C. H., *The Gospel in the New Testament,* (London: The National Sunday School Union, 1929).

3. Walls, Andrew F., "The Gospel as the Prisoner and the Liberator of Culture," Missionalia The South African Missional Society, 10, no. 3 (November 1982): 93–105.

4. Dr. Alexander Maclaren, as quoted in Dr. Selwyn Hughes, *Every Day with Jesus* (England: CWR, Waverly Abbey House, 1997), p. 17-20.

5. Tom Colvin, "Jesu, Jesu" in *The United Methodist Hymnal* (Nashville: The United Methodist Publishing House 1989), 432.

6. McGavran, Donald A., *Discipling Without Dismantling the Tribe, Tongue and People* (Bangalore: Good News Printers, 1998), p. 254.

7. Barna, George, *The Power of Vision: Discover and Apply God's Vision for Your Life and Ministry* (Ventura: Regal From Gospel Light, 2009), p. 26-27.

8. Originally spoken in William Carey's sermon to the Baptist Association Meeting in Northampton, England, May 30, 1792.

9. The Yoido Full Gospel Church, Rev. Dr. David Yonggi Cho.

10. Prayer Mountain is an elevated facility, dedicated and designated

for the purpose of intense prayer and fasting by Christians in South Korea.

11. C. B. Firth, Introduction to Indian Church History (Madras: Christian Literature Society Press, 1961), p. 55-57.

12. Elizabeth O'Connor, *The Eighth Day of Creation: Gifts and Creativity* (Waco: Word Books, 1974), p. 13.

13. *Webster's Dictionary and Thesaurus*, New Landmark: Geddes and Grosset, 2002, 104.

14. Bishop James K. Matthews' speech at the General Conference of The United Methodist Church in India, Madras, November 1989. I was pressent as a delegate at the General Conference of the Methodist Church in India.

For Further Reading

David A. Anderson, *Gracism: The Art of Inclusion*
Lovette H. Weems, Jr., *Focus: The Real Challenges that Face The United Methodist Church*

Contributors

Bishop Linda Lee, now retired, is a graduate of United Theological Seminary (M. Div., D. Min.) in Dayton, Ohio. She served as active layperson in the Dixon United Methodist Church, where she received her call to ministry. Lee served as associate pastor, pastor in charge, and District Superintendent before being elected as the first African American woman bishop in the North Central Jurisdiction of the United Methodist Church. Bishop Lee served as Episcopal Leader in the Michigan Area for four years and in the Wisconsin Area for eight years. Her interest in racial equity has been life long, expressed through her work ecumenically, with the GBCS and as President of GCORR.

Ray Buckley is the interim Director of the Center for Native American Spirituality and Christian Study. He has served The United Methodist Church as a staff member of The United Methodist Publishing House, for nine years as Director of the Native People Communications Office (UMCom), Director of Connectional Ministries and Native Discipleship (Alaska), and a faculty member of The Academy of Spiritual Formation (The Upper Room). The author of eight books, Buckley's stories, poetry, and art have appeared in numerous journals, periodicals, books, and museums around the world. Ray is a traditional basketmaker and woodcarver.

J. Kabamba Kiboko is a clergywoman, published scholar, translator, wife, and mother, born in the Congo, DR and became the first clergywoman ordained in the Southern Congo Conference (1983). Currently, she is Associate Pastor of Holy Covenant UMC and has been serving as Mission Interpreter and Liaison for the Southern

Congo/Zambia Episcopal area since 1986. Delegate to the 1984 General Conference, recently elected member of the Judicial Council, President of the African Clergywomen and has served as a translator at General Conferences since 1992. She holds a Ph.D. in Old Testament with distinction (DU/Iliff School of Theology), M.Div. (Iliff), M.Th. (Perkins); B.A. (Drake), B.Div. (Mulungwishi).

David Maldonado Jr. is a clergy member of the Rio Grande Annual conference in retired status. He is the founding Director of the Center for the Study of Latino/a Christianity and Religions at the Perkins School of Theology, Southern Methodist University and is President Emeritus of Iliff School of Theology (2000–2004). He is the author of *Crossing Guadalupe Street* and the Editor of *Protestantes/Protestants Hispanic Christianity within Mainline Traditions*. Dr. Maldonado has served The United Methodist Church through boards such as the General Board of Higher Education and Ministry, The University Senate, and in other volunteer capacities. He and his wife Charlotte reside in New Mexico.

Åsa Nausner is an Adjunct professor of Communication at Reutlingen School of Theology, Germany. Åsa Nausner grew up in Sweden and nurtured an ecumenical spirit through the World Christian Student Federation during her student years in Lund and Uppsala. International youth exchange with Southern Africa as well as her work as a Christian Educator at Church of Sweden Aid (1990-1998) spurred her interest for international relations and global justice issues. She served as a Director of Christian Education at Madison UMC, New Jersey between 2001 and 2005 and at Pfullingen UMC, Germany between 2006 and 2011. She is part of an UMC European Network for Migrant Ministers and conducts workshops on Intercultural Communication. Åsa Nausner holds a B.A. from Uppsala University, Sweden, a Master of Theological Studies and a PhD (in Social Ethics) from Drew University, Madison, New Jersey, U.S.

Elaine A. Robinson is Academic Dean and Associate Professor of United Methodist Studies and Christian Theology at Saint Paul School of Theology at Oklahoma City University. An ordained elder in the Oklahoma Conference, Dr. Robinson previously taught at Brite Divinity School at Texas Christian University (2000-2008). She attended seminary at Perkins School of Theology and received her Ph.D. from Emory University. Prior to going to seminary, Dr. Robinson served in the U.S. Air Force for ten years. She is the author or co-author of several books and articles including: *These Three: The Theological Virtues of Faith, Hope, and Love* (The Pilgrim Press, 2004); *Considering the Great Commission,* with Stephen Gunter (Abingdon Press, 2005); *Godbearing: Evangelism Reconceived* (The Pilgrim Press, 2006); and *Race and Theology* (Abingdon Press, 2012).

Ross E. Ross is Professor of Religion at Spelman College, Atlanta, Georgia where she led renewal and transformation of the study of religion. An ordained elder in the South Carolina Conference, Ross served pastoral appointments in South Carolina and Georgia. She is author of *Witnessing and Testifying: Black Women, Religion, and Civil Rights, and co-author of The Status of Racial and Ethnic Clergywomen in the United Methodist Church.* Ross is married to the Reverend Ronald S. Bonner. They reside in Atlanta.

Samuel John Royappa, District Superintendent, Capital—Coulee Region of the Wisconsin Annual Conference of the United Methodist Church. Sam Royappa has been in ordained ministry for twenty-eight years—ordained in the Methodist Church in India and transferred to The United Methodist Church, USA. Upon his transfer from the Methodist Church in India to The United Methodist Church in 2000, he served two UM congregations before being appointed as a District Superintendent in 2007. His gifts include missionary leadership, teaching, training, developing multi-cultural/racial congregations, and community-building. He has a B.A. and M.A. from Madurai-Kamaraj University, South India, and Bachelor of Divinity from Serampore University, North India and Doctor of Ministry from Asbury Theological Seminary. He is married to Shanti Samuel with three children.

Safiyah Fosua, consulting editor, is Assistant Professor of Christian Ministry and Congregational Worship at Wesley Seminary at Indiana Wesleyan University in Marion, Indiana. Dr. Fosua, an ordained elder in the UMC, has served as pastor, as missionary to Ghana, and as director of Transformational Preaching ministries at GBOD-UMC. While at GBOD Safiyah was the associate editor of the four-volume *Africana Worship Book* series published by Discipleship Resources (2006-2008). Fosua holds earned degrees from Northwestern University (BA), Oral Roberts University Seminary (M.Div.) and United Theological Seminary in Dayton, Ohio (D.Min). Safiyah is married to the Rev. Dr. Kwasi Kena, also an assistant professor at Wesley Seminary at IWU.

Study Guide

Elaine A. Robinson

General Overview

Christian discipleship begins with one common act: faith in Jesus Christ. That faith—a confidence and trust in the salvific, healing power of God in Jesus Christ—incorporates each of us into the one body of Christ, the invisible communion of all believers. But despite this mystical unity, the church, as a human institution, remains broken and unable to embody fully this unity or oneness in and through Christ. Every time we share in the sacrament of Holy Communion, we confess to God that, "We have failed to be an obedient church. . . . we have rebelled against your loved, we have not loved our neighbor." Too often, our failure to manifest God's love toward one another is rooted in differences in culture, traditions, or language that lead to fear and misunderstanding. We avoid that which we don't understand. We want to shape people in our own image, rather than accepting them as God created them. But it doesn't have to be this way. The church can learn to appreciate and understand more deeply the various cultural expressions in which our Christian faith is lived out. We can learn to sing a new song, to hear the songs of others, and to invite others to join in singing with us. This study invites us to hear the songs of all God's people, to enter into stories of the faithful, and thus to learn more about who we are as The United Methodist Church worshipping in many lands, expressions, and languages.

The scriptures remind us that we human beings share much in common. We are created in the image of God (Gen. 1:27). All are under the condition of sin or separation from God (Rom. 3:9-10).

All are offered the gift of abundant life through faith in Jesus Christ (John 10:10; Rom. 10:12-13). We are all one in Jesus Christ whether Jew or Greek, free or slave, male or female (Gal. 3:28). All nations and peoples will be held accountable to God (Matt. 25:31-46). All share the common hope of a good future in and through God's love (John 3:16). We share much in common, especially as disciples of Jesus Christ.

Yet our differences cannot be minimized. As Paul wrote to the Corinthians, the people of God are created with different gifts and abilities, as determined by the Holy Spirit (1 Cor. 12:4-11). We speak different languages. We worship God in different ways. We have distinct musical traditions and customs for gathering together. The Book of Acts reminds us that at Pentecost, different languages were spoken and affirmed. In his sermon, "The Lord Our Righteousness," John Wesley urged that we should "think and let think" when it comes to differences of opinions such as ways of worshiping or speaking, so long as we have faith in Jesus Christ who offers the forgiveness of sin and receive the Holy Spirit's gift of transforming love. In other words, we should express unity in the essentials of the faith and allow for variations in "opinions" or non-essentials.

Today, The United Methodist Church, as a global body, grows ever more diverse. Likewise, the global community becomes increasingly mobile and interconnected through social media, communications, and transportation. As a result, we have the opportunity to learn from one another like never before in human history. We, the church, can step out in faith and live into our oneness in Christ. We can encourage others to live fully human lives as God intended, rather than insisting on imposing our own cultural standards on others. We can enable the healing power of Christ to renew our churches and transform the world. And as we step out in faith, we may find that, by grace, we have been shaped and conformed into a living expression of beloved community.

Instructions for Group Facilitators and Participants

This study guide encourages the people of God to encounter the experiences of United Methodists in different cultural contexts. In today's world, intercultural competence and compassion is more important than ever before. As followers of Jesus Christ, we need to be skilled at embracing our common humanity while respecting different cultures, races, and ethnicities. To facilitate this group study and our encounter with different cultural experiences, several considerations should be kept in mind:

1. Before the first session, participants should read Bishop Linda Lee's Introduction, as well as this General Introduction and Instructions for Group Facilitators and Participants.
2. Encourage the group to read and reflect upon each assigned chapter before the class meeting. This group study and the discussions depend upon a careful engagement with each of the chapters.
3. While reading, participants should remain open to the experience of each writer, without challenging or questioning that experience, on the one hand, or denying or denigrating it, on the other. Let each person speak from his or her own life experiences and faith, listening in Christian love. The writers' aim is neither to point fingers nor to suggest that the author's experience is that of the entire ethnic or racial group, but simply to speak the truth in love as he or she has lived the Christian faith.
4. Begin and end each group session in prayer. There is no substitute for inviting the gentle presence of the Holy Spirit to illuminate our hearts and minds.
5. Don't pick and choose among the chapters, but honor them all. Include every author in your study as a brother or sister in Christ.
6. It is not necessary to answer all of the discussion questions, but don't avoid difficult topics. Rather, offer them to God and seek the inspiration of the Holy Spirit as you consider them.
7. If the conversation should become emotionally charged, invite everyone into a few moments of silent meditation. Focus on the breath of God as it sustains the gift of life. Pray together for the love of Christ to provide the peace that surpasses all understanding.
8. Each chapter offers resources for further study, which the group might want to consult or use for conversation beyond

the pages of this study document. The resources are intended to allow us to go deeper, if desired.

9. Finally, believe that God's grace has the power to bring us closer together as one body in Christ expressed through our global United Methodist Church. By faith, we can become the beloved community in visible form.

Introduction

Bishop Linda Lee

Preparation: Read the General Introduction, Instructions for Group Facilitators and Participants, and Bishop Lee's Introduction.

Questions for Group Discussion:

1. Why should our local congregations be concerned about people who seem to be different from us?

2. What does the Bible say about our human commonalities?

3. What was your experience of racial and ethnic differences growing up? Have your views changed through the course of your lifetime? Share a story of experiencing God's grace through someone from a different cultural background than your own.

4. What do the words of Paul Lawrence Dunbar mean to you? What might they mean in the context of your local congregation?

5. The Council of Bishops 2011 statement calls us to act intentionally with compassion and to overcome evil with good in order to further the existence of beloved community. What would beloved community look like and feel like? Share a story that illustrates your experience of or hope for beloved community.

6. What would you like to see happen as result of this group study?

One: *Tiospaye,* Brothers and Sisters, Listen Carefully

Ray Buckley

Preparation: Read the chapter by Ray Buckley. Visit the website for the national Native American Comprehensive Plan of The United Methodist Church at http://www.gbod.org/site/c.nhLRJ2PMKsG/b.4751535/k.9027/Native_American.htm

Questions for Group Discussion:

1. What does Buckley mean by the phrase "Standing-with-Nothing-Between? How does this understanding create a sense of belovedness?

2. Buckley shares that Native cultures speak of Mitaque oyasin or "all my relations." What new insights do you find in this description of relationship? Share an experience or story in which you experienced this sense of relationship.

3. What does the author mean when he writes, "Tolerance is racism on hold"?

4. What happened at Sand Creek? What were the sources or conditions that allowed this massacre to occur? Why might the process of healing the church begin here?

5. Buckley shares the social realities that undermine the lives of Native Americans and suggests that active racism contributes directly to these conditions. What might be done, especially by the church, to change the nature and impact of active racism?

6. Buckley writes, "The poor have received the gospel but are unable to keep it, practice it, or regularly engage in the intimacies

of community." In what ways has the gospel been offered to indigenous people and yet not maintained once the people become disciples of Jesus Christ?

7. What does it mean to be a disciple of Jesus Christ, according to Buckley?

8. What one thing from this chapter will reshape or deepen your faith and discipleship?

Two: A Tapestry in the Disanga: Building Beloved Community from a Congolese Perspective

Kabamba Kiboko

Preparation: Read "A Tapestry in the Disanga: Building Beloved Community from a Congolese Perspective" by J. Kabamba Kiboko. Visit one of the following websites to learn more about the Democratic Republic of Congo: http://www.state.gov/r/pa/ei/bgn/2823.htm or http://www.unhcr.org/pages/49e45c366.html. Visit the UMC website for information on the African conferences and Episcopal areas: http://archives.umc.org/interior.asp?mid=5889

Questions for Discussion:

1. What does "Disanga" mean? How does it set the framework for Kiboko's understanding of beloved community?

2. Kiboko notes that she has served an Anglo congregation and an African American congregation. How would your church respond to the appointment of a Musanga clergywoman as its pastor? Why would this be the church's response?

3. Does the Basanga understanding of God seem strange to you or does it remind you of the God you know and worship? Are there biblical verses that resonate with the Basanga description?

4. According to Kiboko, the Basanga view religion as relating to all aspects of life. Do you view your Christian faith in similar terms?

5. Without making value judgments about the Basanga way of life, what strikes you as similar to your cultural standards and what seems most different?

6. How would you describe the "complex layers" of racism within the African context?

7. How might the story from Bishop Muzorewa be refashioned and retold from within your cultural context?

8. Why do you think the terms for African bishops differ from those of U.S. bishops? Does this seem fair and appropriate?

9. How does the Old Testament envision the beloved community? And how could the global church bear witness to beloved community in the midst of the situation faced by the Democratic Republic of Congo?

10. What one thing from this chapter will reshape or deepen your faith and discipleship?

Three: Building Beloved Community: The Church in the Midst of Racism, A U.S. Latino/Hispanic Perspective

David Maldonado Jr.

Preparation: Read "Building Beloved Community: The Church within the Midst of Racism" by David Maldonado, Jr. Visit the website for the National Plan for Hispanic/Latino Ministries at http://new.gbgm-umc.org/plan/hispanic/

Questions for Group Discussion:

1. Maldonado states that "although the Latino population predates white settlements within the boundaries of the present United States, it is traditionally perceived as a foreign and immigrant population." Why do you think Latinos/as are viewed in this way? Does the church contribute to this perception or help to change it?

2. How have the notions of Manifest Destiny and the "superiority" of Anglo Americans contributed to racist attitudes within The United Methodist Church?

3. Does the church seem to undermine the building of beloved community in relation to Hispanic Americans and immigrants? What might we do differently as people of God?

4. What does Maldonado mean by "quiet racism" in today's church?

5. What insights into beloved community are provided by the Ten Commandments?

6. Maldonado offers several signs of hope that building beloved community is possible. Which of his signs do you find most promising or helpful?

7. What one thing from this chapter will reshape or deepen your faith and discipleship?

Four: Becoming Beloved Communities in Europe—A Challenge to Expand Our Comfort Zones

Åsa Nausner

Preparation: Read Åsa Nausner's chapter, "Beloved Communities in Europe—A Challenge to Expand Our Comfort Zones!" Visit the website www.umc-europe.org and www.emk.de to learn more about United Methodism in Europe.

Questions for Group Discussion:

1. Nausner introduces the Swedish word, lagom. What does lagom mean and how might it point to beloved community? At the same time, how might lagom prevent the creation of beloved community?

2. What does it suggest that "there was a time when a Swede on a train could look around the coach guessing what every one was having for dinner, and be right about it"?

3. Growing up, Nausner's father was forbidden from interacting with Roma people (sometimes known as Gypsies). In your childhood, were there groups of people with whom you were not to interact? Why? Does this continue to be the case today or has it changed?

4. How would you characterize the shape of Christian faith in Sweden? How is it similar to or different from your own experience?

5. Nausner points to Matthew 25 to suggest that we are to meet and listen to the stranger in our midst. If you were to take this idea

seriously, who would be the strangers your congregation should meet and listen to? Are there some people you meet with silence?

6. When her African American friend visited Europe, Nausner became aware that her city had racism she had not seen before. Where do you think racism might be hiding in your own community or church that you have not yet recognized?

7. A recent newspaper article claimed that "Sweden would come to a halt without immigrants." Why is this the case? Are there other countries or communities that could also make this claim?

8. Nausner shares the experience of a Scandinavian pastor who is leading an intercultural congregation. Why do you think diverse people are joining this congregation? How might your own congregation be willing to learn from others and change some of its own practices to become a living sign of the beloved community?

9. What one thing from this chapter will reshape or deepen your faith and discipleship?

Five: New Eyes to See

Elaine A. Robinson

Preparation: Read "New Eyes to See" by Elaine Robinson. Consult the General Commission on Religion and Race website at www.gcorr.org.

Questions for Group Discussion:

1. What does Robinson mean by her own "Damascus Road" experience? Can you relate to this notion of being given new eyes to see?

2. Robinson refers to "white privilege." Have you experienced or been aware of white privilege in your own life?

3. What is systemic sin? Can you think of biblical or societal examples of systemic sin?

4. The stories of Babel and Pentecost speak of God's creation of unity in diversity. How might these biblical stories help us understand and create beloved community in our own time?

5. What is repentance? How might repentance of racism lead us toward healing and wholeness as a church?

6. Robinson tells the story of a member of her church in Texas who related his immigration experience to the book of Ruth. When has the Bible come alive for you because you have seen it through someone else's eyes?

7. How can majority culture people become more attuned to the cultures of persons of other races and ethnicities and the "double consciousness" they live with?

8. What does it mean to be called by God to dismantle racism? How can a Christian or a congregation fulfill a calling such as this?

9. What one thing from this chapter will reshape or deepen your faith and discipleship?

Six: Becoming a Beloved Community: An African American Perspective

Rosetta E. Ross

Preparation: Read Rosetta E. Ross' chapter, "Becoming Beloved Community: An African American Perspective." Visit the website http://new.gbgm-umc.org/resources/annual/blackhistorymonth or learn more about the former Central Jurisdiction at http://archives.umc.org/interior.asp?ptid=2&mid=6723

Questions for Group Discussion:

1. Ross describes the brokenness of communities in South Carolina. How would you describe this kind of brokenness in your own community? What is the source of such brokenness?

2. What would the vision of Acts 4 and 5 look like if it were lived out in your own church and community?

3. According to Ross, what does the Bible tell us about broken community?

4. Ross points to the "deceptions" that exist in relation to theories of racism. What are these deceptions? Do you think they exist within your own community? How might you find out?

5. How would you describe Methodism's "legacy" on race?

6. What one thing from this chapter will reshape or deepen your faith and discipleship?

Seven: From God-Community to a Beloved Community

Samuel John Royappa

Preparation: Read the Chapter by Sam Royappa. Visit the website for the Asian American Comprehensive Plan for the United Methodist Church at new.gbgm-umc.org/plan/asianamerican/ and the World Council of Churches' website for basic information on the Methodist Church in India: http://www.oikoumene.org/en/member-churches/regions/asia/india/methodist-church-in-india.html

Questions for Group Discussion:

1. Drawing upon biblical sources, the author develops the term "God-community." How does this understanding relate to what we know as the church?

2. According to Royappa, what were the five features of the first faith community? Do you recognize these features in your own congregation?

3. What compels us to be in mission to all peoples? How does diversity relate to God's mission in the world?

4. What is the caste system in India? Have you experienced anything that might resemble a caste system in your country?

5. What does the author suggest we can do to develop cross-cultural and cross-racial ministries?

6. What does contextualization mean? What might it mean for your own church and the community in which you live?

7. What one thing from this chapter will reshape or deepen your faith and discipleship?

Conclusion: Becoming Beloved Community

Preparation: Skim the chapters again and the points that have deepened your faith and understanding. Read the concluding comments below.

We all live in the midst of multiple cultures. Some of us live in rural settings, others in large urban contexts. Some of us are most comfortable in the culture of the South, while others feel at home in the Midwest, the Northeast, or on the West Coast. Some of us are in Europe, Africa, the Philippines, Central or South America, Near East or Far East. Even our individual congregations have certain "cultures" or ways of doing things and understanding life together and the world in which we exercise our faith. We also live in a time when racial and ethnic diversity is an inescapable part of our lives. It is the world that God created. It is also the world that human hands have shaped.

As Christians, we believe that Jesus Christ has come to offer life abundant to all people and to bring the kingdom of God into the world. As followers of Jesus Christ, we are called to be agents of God's love and transforming power in the midst of a broken world. We are called to be Christ's hands and heart in helping to foster beloved community in the places where we live and worship. In this final session, our task is to consider how our local congregations might become more interculturally compassionate and grow as an expression of beloved community.

Questions for Group Discussion:

1. What have been the common threads arising throughout your study of these essays? How is God at work in what you have learned?

2. In what ways is your congregation able to navigate different cultures? Where do you think the Holy Spirit is leading you to grow?

3. Name one or two tangible actions your group or congregation can take to deepen your intercultural skills and to become more fully a representation of the beloved community of Jesus Christ.

4. 1 Peter 3:15 reminds us: "Whenever anyone asks you to speak of your hope, be ready to defend it." How would you express your hope in the possibility and reality of beloved community?

For Further Reading

Council of Bishops of The United Methodist Church, 2011 Statement online at http://www.umc.org/atf/cf/%7Bdb6a45e4-c446-4248-82c8-e131b6424741%7D/BELOVED_COMMUNITY_STATEMENT.PDF

Abrahams, Ivan. "To Serve the Present Age, Our Calling to Fulfill," in *Our Calling to Fulfill*. Nashville: Kingswood Books, 2009. [Abrahams is the Bishop of the Methodist Church of South Africa.]

Anderson, David A., *Gracism: The Art of Inclusion*.

Barton, Paul. "Inter-Ethnic Relations between Mexican American and Anglo American Methodists in the U.S. Southwest 1836-1938," in *Protestantes/Protestants*. Nashville: Abingdon Press, 1999.

Bass, Diana Butler, *Christianity for the Rest of Us: How the Neighborhood Church Is Transforming the Faith*.

Brueggemann, Walter. *Journey to the Common Good*. Louisville, KY: Westminster John Knox Press, 2010.

Cone, James H. *The Cross and the Lynching Tree*. Maryknoll, NY: Orbis Books, 2011.

Deymaz, Mark. *Building a Healthy Multi-Ethnic Church*.

DeYoung, Curtis Paul. *Radical Reconciliation: Beyond Political Pietism and Christian Quietism*.

Fassett, Thom. White Wolf. *Giving Our Hearts Away: Native American Survival. United Methodist Women*, 2008.

González, Justo, editor. *Each in Our Own Tongue: A History of Hispanic United Methodism*. Nashville: Abingdon Press, 1991.

Greenlee, David. *One Cross One Way Many Journeys: Thinking Again About Conversion*.

Hall, Ron and Denver Moore. *Same Kind of Different as Me*. Nashville: Thomas Nelson, 2006.

Innis, John G. *By the Goodness of God: An Autobiography*. Nashville: Abingdon Press, 2003. [Innis is the United Methodist Bishop of Liberia.]

Kivel, Paul. *Uprooting Racism*. Canada: New Society Publishers, 2011

Law, Eric. *Inclusion: Making Room for Grace*. Chalice Press, 2000.

Langbehn, Volker and Mohammad Salama. *German Colonialism: Race, the Holocaust and Postwar Germany*. New York: Columbia University Press, 2011.

Ernest S. Lyght, Ernest S., Glory E. Dharmaraj, and Jacob S, Dharmaraj. *Many Faces One Church: A Manual for Cross-Racial and Cross Cultural Ministry*.

Maldonado, David, *Crossing Guadalupe Street: Growing Up Hispanic and Protestant*,

Martinez, Juan. *Sea La Luz*. University of North Texas Press.

McIntosh, Peggy. "White Privilege: Unpacking the Invisible Knapsack," in *White Privilege*, edited by Paula S. Rothenberg. New York: Worth Publishers, 2008. [McIntosh's essay is widely available online.]

Noley, Homer. *First White Frost: Native Americans and United Methodism*. Nashville: Abingdon Press, 1991.

Perkinson, James W. *White Theology*. New York: Palgrave Macmillan, 2004.

Pred, Allen. Even in *Sweden: Racisms, Racialized Spaces, and the Popular Geographical*

Robinson, Elaine. *Race and Theology*. Nashville: Abingdon Press, 2012.

Schulz, Katherine. *A Framework to Teaching Across Differences*, New York: Teachers Collage Press, 2003.

Shockley, Grant S., editor. *Heritage and Hope: The African American Presence in United Methodism*. Nashville: Abingdon Press, 1991.

Sow, Noah. *Deutschland Schwarz Weiss: Der Alltagliche Rassismus*, Munchen: C. Bethelsmann Verlan, 2008. [The title translates as: Germany Black—White—Daily Racism.]

Streiff, Patrick. *Methodism in Europe: 19th and 20th Century*. Baltic Methodist Theological Seminary, 2003. [Streiff is the United Methodist Bishop of Central and Southern Europe.]

Thandeka. *Learning to be White: Money, Race and God in America*. New York: Continuum, 1999.

Thomas, Donna S. *Faces in the Crowd: Reaching Your International Neighbor for Christ*.

Thomas, James. *Methodism's Racial Dilemma: The Story of the Central Jurisdiction*. Nashville: Abingdon Press, 1992.

Weems, Jr., Lovett H. *Focus: The Real Challenges That Face The United Methodist Church*, Allan Aubrey Boesak, MaryKnoll, NY: Orbis Books, 2012.

Made in the USA
Middletown, DE
15 February 2015